POLITICAL PHILOSOPHY NOW

Chief Editor of the Series:
Howard Williams, University of Wales, Aberystwyth

Associate Editors:
Wolfgang Kersting, University of Kiel, Germany
Steven B. Smith, Yale University, USA
Peter Nicholson, University of York, England
Renato Cristi, Wilfrid Laurier University, Waterloo, Canada

Political Philosophy Now is a series which deals with authors, topics and periods in political philosophy from the perspective of their relevance to current debates. The series presents a spread of subjects and points of view from various traditions which include European and New World debates in political philosophy.

For other titles in this series, please see the University of Wales Press website: *www.wales.ac.uk/press*

POLITICAL PHILOSOPHY NOW

Ideology: Contemporary Social, Political and Cultural Theory

Robert Porter

UNIVERSITY OF WALES PRESS • CARDIFF • 2006

© Robert Porter, 2006

British Library Cataloguing-in-Publication Data
A catalogue record for this book is available from the British Library.

ISBN 0-7083-1865-7 hardback
0-7083-1864-9 paperback

All rights reserved. No part of this book may be reproduced, stored in a retrieval system, or transmitted, in any form or by any means, electronic, mechanical, photocopying, recording or otherwise, without clearance from the University of Wales Press, 10 Columbus Walk, Brigantine Place, Cardiff, CF10 4UP.
www.wales.ac.uk/press

The right of Robert Porter to be identified as author of this work has been asserted by him in accordance with sections 77 and 78 of the Copyright, Designs and Patents Act 1988.

Printed in Great Britain by Cromwell Press Ltd, Trowbridge, Wiltshire

For

Kerry-Ann, Jessica and Anna – 'the girls'

Contents

Acknowledgements		ix
1	Introducing the Critical Conception of Ideology	1
2	Habermas's Ideology Theory	18
3	Habermas's Moral Critique of Ideology	36
4	Žižek's Ideology Theory	52
5	Žižek's Ethical Critique of Ideology	72
6	Deleuze's Ideology Theory	86
7	Deleuze's Ethical Critique of Ideology	103
8	Conclusion	117
Notes		138
Bibliography		154
Index		159

Acknowledgements

This book grew out of thesis work that I began nearly ten years ago and, as a consequence, I have amassed many debts along the way. As both an undergraduate and graduate student in the School of Politics at Queens University Belfast I benefited from the insights and wisdom of many of my teachers. For helping me begin to negotiate the difficult terrain of contemporary social, political and cultural theory I am particularly grateful to Alan Finlayson and Shane O'Neill. For deepening my understanding of the stakes involved in the activity of social, political and cultural criticism, for providing supportive, stimulating and challenging Ph.D. supervision, and for continuing to engage with and enliven my work, I am extremely grateful and happy to acknowledge my huge intellectual debt to Iain Mackenzie.

If this book grew out of work I began at Queens, then it matured and came to fruition during my time at the University of Ulster. Many in the School of Media and Performing Arts, the Centre For Media Research and the Media Studies Research Institute have helped me sharpen my critical tools in a research environment that is as congenial and exciting as any I have experienced. I have benefited from conversations and engagements with the following friends and colleagues at Ulster: Maire Messenger-Davies, Martin McLoone, Dan Fleming, Paul Moore, Andy White, Andrew Hill, Aphra Kerr, Ned Rossiter and Daniel Jewesbury. More particularly, I would like to acknowledge a debt of gratitude to John Hill, whose intellectual generosity and pluralism were crucial in helping me to see this work through to its conclusion.

Richard Houdmont, Nia Peris and Sarah Lewis from University of Wales Press generously gave of their time in support of this project. I am particularly grateful to Sarah, whose professionalism, humanity and good humour never waned in the face of an anxious first-time academic author. For crucial scholarly advice and guidance at both the beginning and the end of the project, and for forcing me to think a little harder about what I was trying to do, I am especially indebted to Howard Williams. In this regard, I would also like to thank the two anonymous readers for their critical and constructive comments on the manuscript.

Lastly, and most importantly, I want to acknowledge the love and support of my family. For shouldering a significant amount of the childcare responsibilities that became ours after the birth of our first daughter, and for providing me with the autonomy and space to begin writing the book, I am extremely grateful to Ann and Derek Gilmore. My grandfather, William Cardwell, introduced me to the world of books, stimulating the intellectual curiosity that continues to define me as a person. My daughters, Jessica and Anna, are such a source of joy and fun and each, in their own way, have taught me – and will no doubt continue to teach me – the critical importance of looking at the world in new and different ways. My wife, Kerry-Ann, is a constant source of love, support and commitment. This book is dedicated to her and my two daughters – 'the girls'.

1 • Introducing the Critical Conception of Ideology

The guiding theme or concern of this book will be to explore the possibility of developing a *critical conception of ideology*, or to map certain conditions and elucidate some key animating features of a *critique of ideology*. But what, we immediately need to ask, would such a critical conception of ideology look like? Or, to pose the same question in a slightly different fashion, what will the term 'critique of ideology' come to signify in this context? In order to make sense of these questions or address these issues I will draw on the work of three influential figures in contemporary social, political and cultural theory: Jürgen Habermas, Slavoj Žižek and Gilles Deleuze. Each of these thinkers will offer us a way of thinking about ideology in explicitly and resolutely critical terms. That is to say, Habermas, Žižek and Deleuze will provide us with three images or ways of picturing what a 'critical conception of ideology' would look like; three different forms of ideology critique. Now, although these different pictures or images will vary in tone, texture and affect, they will nonetheless be framed in accordance with two common themes or intuitions which will emerge and begin to predominant in the pages and chapters to follow. The first theme concerns the relationship between the real and the ideological or, better still, the issue of how we are to theorize the relation between ideology and the real. We shall see that Habermas, Žižek and Deleuze all insist on the intuition that a distinction can be drawn between the real and the ideological, and that the critique of ideology implied in their thought is anchored by an intuitive reliance on what we can call a non-ideological or pre-ideological real. And the second theme concerns how we are to theorize the relation between ideology and the moral or ethical. Here we shall see that the critique of ideology to be found in Habermas, Žižek and Deleuze always or necessarily proceeds on certain moral or ethical grounds. These, then, are the two core intuitions at play in the critical conception of ideology, and it is these core animating features of the critique of ideology that will be extrapolated from the thought of Habermas, Žižek and Deleuze.

It will prove useful, by way of this first or introductory chapter, to take each of these core intuitions or themes and provide, in relatively broad terms, an initial sense of how they will be subsequently mapped out. In the first part of the chapter, I will focus on the question of how to theorize the relation between the real and the ideological. Before coming to anticipate the specific ways in which Habermas, Deleuze and Žižek think through this issue, it is important to acknowledge that theorizations concerning how the ideological relates to the real are as old and as contestable as the concept of ideology itself. In light of this consideration, I will spend a little time engaging with the classical and contemporary ideology theory of thinkers such as Antoine Destutt de Tracy, Marx and Engels, Paul Ricoeur and Michael Freeden. Two main points will emerge from this discussion. Firstly, we shall see that a certain line of continuity persists between the classical ideology theory of Marx and Engels and that of Habermas, Žižek and Deleuze, such that we could say that they all insist that a critical distinction can be drawn between the ideological and the real (albeit on different terms). Second, we shall see that influential figures in contemporary ideology theory such as Ricoeur and Freeden would want to put a clear question mark against this suggestion by emphasizing how the real is, in effect, always-already ideological. In the second part of the chapter, I anticipate the moral or ethical terms on which Habermas's, Žižek's and Deleuze's respective critiques of ideology proceed, while also raising some possible problems or difficulties with the intuition that the critique of ideology always or necessarily proceeds on certain moral or ethical grounds. In the third and final part of the chapter, I will give a more specific, if rather brief, indication of how the book will be structured, or, better still, how its argument will subsequently unfold and gather momentum chapter by chapter.

The real and the ideological

Let us start, then, by thinking about the question of how to theorize the relation between the real and the ideological. The first point to stress is, as I have just indicated, that theorizations concerning how the ideological relates to the real are as old and as contestable as the concept of ideology itself. We can go right back, for example, to the thinker who is often credited with first employing the term 'ideology': namely, Antoine Destutt de Tracy. Writing in the late eighteenth century, de Tracy suggested that ideology could be thought of as a kind of scientific method, a 'science of ideas' to be progressively employed for the betterment of political society as a whole. Put simply, de Tracy believed that a scientific study of ideas could foster a better understanding of the human condition such that social relations could be arranged to materially reflect real human aspirations, desires and needs. In this way, ideology, as a 'science of ideas', is grounded in the real, where the 'real' is intuitively theorized as the human condition itself, or as a form of human nature that is perfectible and amenable to systematic analysis.[1] Of course, and in a twist that was as tragicomic as it was sudden, de Tracy's initial conception of ideology underwent a rather dramatic reversal as the notion assumed a contradictory meaning to the one he intended.[2] First, in the hands of Napoleon, and then ever more systematically and famously in the hands of Marx and Engels, the concept of ideology began to assume a meaning or resonance that was far from progressive and enlightened. Napoleon engaged in a series of polemical diatribes and attacks against, what he disparagingly called, the 'shadowy metaphysics' of de Tracy and the other members of his intellectual and political circle. From Napoleon's perspective, the notion of ideology as a 'science of ideas' was both pretentious and potentially damaging in that it remained abstracted from the real, rather than grounded in it. That is to say, 'ideologues' such as de Tracy abstracted themselves from the practical realities of political life and insisted on developing fanciful theories that were both doctrinaire and impractical in equal measure.[3]

While Napoleon's critique of de Tracy's concept of ideology is far from unproblematic, not least because it reflected a rather opportunistic attempt to consolidate his power and attack ideas that may have been disruptive of his hegemony in France at that time,[4] he nonetheless expressed an intuition that echoes down to the present day. For his claim is that those who labour under ideology are, in some fundamental sense, flawed in their outlook, that they do not understand the real or the realities of social and political life. By way of this mode of thinking, ideology is cut adrift from the real or, better still, ideology implies a blinkered obscurantism that grips us and prevents us from developing an adequate consciousness of the real. Of course, the most exemplary, original and influential articulation of this idea of ideology is to be found in Marx and Engels. Marx and Engels, writing in the mid-nineteenth century, take what is expressed only as an opportunistic impulse in Napoleon and reconstruct it as part of a new comprehensive theoretical system. Like Napoleon, Marx and Engels employ the term ideology in a polemical fashion, but unlike Napoleon they also attempt to explain the social conditions in which ideology emerges as such. How do they do this? Consider the – now famous and often quoted – passage from their path-breaking and hugely influential book *The German Ideology*:

> Men are the producers of their conceptions, ideas, etc. – real active men, as they are conditioned by a definite development of their productive forces and of the intercourse corresponding to these, up to its furthest forms. Consciousness can never be anything else than conscious existence, and the existence of men is their actual life process. If in ideology men and their circumstances appear up-side down as in a *camera obscura*, this phenomenon arises just as much from their historical life process as the inversion of objects on the retina does from their physical life process.[5]

So we see that for Marx and Engels ideology operates in a way that distorts or inverts the way we look at the social world, essentially stopping us from developing a real or adequate understanding of the 'circumstances' in which we find ourselves. Now, if, under the grip of ideology, we perceive things in a distorted manner, in an 'up-side down' fashion, this is not merely because of any lack of intellect or faulty reasoning on our part. For we are, Marx and Engels want to argue, inevitably caught up in ideology to the extent that we remain essentially unconscious of the fact that the real material conditions of social life – the 'actual life process' or 'historical life process' as they call it – actually shape how we think, conceive, feel and ultimately act. Of course, what Marx and Engels have in mind here is the role the economy plays in shaping the development and exchange of ideas in social life, and how it governs the meanings that we invest in the social. Or, to make the point more explicit, Marx and Engels stress the importance of economic class relations, and, in particular, the power and influence of the ruling or dominant class in modern capitalist society – the 'bourgeoisie' – to disseminate and rationalize ideas that are tailored to suit their economic or material interests. In this way, then, the function of ideology is to give intellectual, moral and political currency to a deliberately distorted vision of social reality that ensures the dominance of specific class interests. Again we can quote from *The German Ideology*:

> The class which has the means of material production at its disposal has control at the same time over the means of mental production, so that

INTRODUCING THE CRITICAL CONCEPTION OF IDEOLOGY 5

thereby . . . the ideas of those who lack the means of mental production are subject to it. The ruling ideas are nothing more than the ideal expression of the dominant material relationships, the dominant material relationships grasped as ideas; hence of the relationships which make one class the ruling one . . .[6]

While there has been much debate and disagreement among scholars and students of ideology concerning how best to understand the legacy of Marx and Engels, there is little doubt of their influence over subsequent generations of ideology theorists.[7] This of course is not to say that their work has gone uncontested, or their arguments unchallenged. Indeed, if we move from the mid-nineteenth century to contemporary intellectual culture or debates, we can see clearly the extent to which Marx and Engels's theory of ideology has come under critical scrutiny and we can see, more particularly for our purposes, how their notions of the real and the ideological sit ill at ease with some influential figures in contemporary ideology theory. Two influential figures or thinkers will suffice for illustrative purposes here: Paul Ricoeur and Michael Freeden. Both Ricoeur and Freeden would find it hard to accept the way in which Marx and Engels theorize the relation between the real and the ideological. As was implied above, Marx and Engels insist on a clear and substantive distinction between the real and the ideological, where the 'real' is understood as the real material or economic conditions of social life, and where the 'ideological' is understood to be the circulation of ideas in the service of dominant class interests. So why, then, from Ricoeur's or Freeden's perspective is this Marxian argument unacceptable?

Let us focus first on Ricoeur. The Marxian approach to ideology is problematic to the degree that it assumes a notion of the 'real' that is taken to be clearly distinct and somehow independent or autonomous from the ideological. Put simply, for Ricoeur the real is not distinct from the ideological, the real *is* ideological, or, better still, the ideological importantly conditions the real. We can begin to see why this is so if we consider the following passage from Ricoeur's well-known essay 'Science and ideology':

> The interpretative code of an ideology is something in *which* men live and think, rather than a conception *that* they pose. In other words, an ideology is operative and not thematic. It operates behind our backs, rather than appearing as a theme before our eyes. We think from it rather than about it.[8]

So we see that for Ricoeur ideology is immediately thought of as an 'interpretative code' that remains operative 'behind our backs'; that we always 'think from' rather than 'think about' ideology. An important consequence of the 'non-transparence' of ideology, as Ricoeur would say, is that our sense of the real (where the 'real' is understood as the interpretative meanings that social actors invest in their shared social reality) is always-already ideological. In other words, it is impossible to have or develop an interpretative sense of a shared social reality without drawing on a cultural code that is, in some way, ideologically pre-constituted, and, as such, beyond conscious critical scrutiny. Take, to use an example actually employed by Ricoeur, the American Declaration of Independence. This interpretative code exercises a decisive ideological influence on US political society as it embodies certain values – that is, individualism, freedom, equal rights and so on – that, by and large, remain unquestioned. That many different social and political actors interpret these values differently, and argue about how best to ensure their observance, precisely shows how the values themselves are fundamental to the self-understandings of those who share this social space, or who belong to this community. Put simply, these values are part and parcel of the reality of what it means to be a US citizen.[9] The temptation here, undoubtedly, would be to insist on the possibility of obtaining some critical distance from the undue influence of the cultural and ideological codes that are predominant in the social world that we inhabit, to develop some critical consciousness of how our position in the social is governed by the operation of dominant or hegemonic values. While Ricoeur would certainly not discount the possibility of such a critique of ideology, he would nonetheless caution us to remember that the forms of critical knowledge we develop about the social are necessarily 'partial' and 'fragmentary'. And the reason for this is that the knowledge of our position and relations in society is always-already conditioned by a kind of social 'belonging' that is spatially-temporally particular and 'non-transparent'. Or, in Ricoeur's own words:

> All objectifying knowledge about our position in society . . . is preceded by a relation of belonging upon which we can never entirely reflect. Before any critical distance, we belong to a history, to a class, to a nation, to a culture, to one or several traditions . . .[10]

Ricoeur wants to make clear that our knowledge of the social world is restricted by the contingencies of social 'belonging' – that is, our being

INTRODUCING THE CRITICAL CONCEPTION OF IDEOLOGY 7

thrown into a particular social 'tradition' – which ideologically shapes our reflections from the very first moment. Or, to put it another way, ideology is already thought to be contingently part of the sense-creating activities of actors who seek to attribute sense and significance to any shared social reality. This brings us neatly to the ideology theory of Michael Freeden. Like Ricoeur, Freeden is at pains to emphasize the contingency of the meanings through which ideology, or competing ideologies, takes shape. Now the shape or, what Freeden calls, 'morphology' of any given ideological perspective on the social is necessarily conditioned by the 'political concepts' through which it is mediated, and, consequently, legitimized. In this regard, the theorist or 'student', as Freeden prefers, of ideology must foster a critical appreciation of how political concepts can ideologically function by ordering the social and political world in certain specific ways. As Freeden himself puts it in his comprehensive and impressive *Ideologies and Political Theory*:

> competing ideologies are . . . struggles over the socially legitimate meanings of the political concepts and the sustaining arrangements they form, in an attempt to establish a 'correct' usage . . . What is meaningful *is* why one specific . . . ordering of the political world prevails over another.[11]

Extrapolating slightly from Freeden here, we can say that ideologies operate by way of a struggle for recognition, where 'recognition' implies an 'ordering of the political' in accordance with 'concepts' that are taken and accepted as inherently 'meaningful'. Say, for example, I wanted to argue that David Fincher's much talked-about and popular film *Fight Club* (1999) offers us a significant and trenchant leftist critique of consumer capitalism.[12] *Fight Club*, I could more specifically suggest, draws attention to the fact that the value-system of consumer capitalism is a hollow and meaningless sham, contradictory in nature and repressive in function. There is a key scene in the film where this particular intuition is palpably expressed and reinforced. Here we find Tyler Durden, the central figure or character, giving a rallying speech which is intended to politicize his fellow members of the fight club by explicitly encouraging them to resist the value-system of consumer capitalism – that is, he cautions them to wake up to the fact that consumerism promises a life of recognition and significance, while only delivering crummy jobs that enable nothing, save the further consumption of essentially meaningless or useless products and goods. 'Advertising', Durden caustically remarks during this speech, 'has us chasing cars and clothes; working jobs we hate so we can buy shit we don't need!' Now, coming back to Freeden or from Freeden's point of view, this argument or interpretation of *Fight Club* can be understood as 'ideological' precisely because it can be analysed in terms of the 'political concepts' through which it is set up or assembled; namely, *Fight Club's* expression and critique of 'consumer capitalism' as 'hollow', 'contradictory' and 'repressive'. Further, this particular assemblage of concepts or ideological argument becomes significant and 'meaningful' to the extent that it 'prevails' over others; say, the argument that *Fight Club* actually reflects a certain 'crisis' in masculinity; or that it essays the 'monstrous thrill' or seductive nature of violence.[13] In this way, the social and political 'meaning' to be taken from *Fight Club* is, in Freeden's terms, 'ideologically decontested' in so far as it is unquestionably recognized as the best or most adequate way of reading the text or film in question.[14]

It is necessary to stress, as Freeden consistently does, that ideologies are also constantly subject to interrogation and contestation: that decontested meanings can be rendered contestable and can be reshaped accordingly. This is obviously implied by the possible alternative readings of *Fight Club* suggested above. And the reason that different political readings of *Fight Club* can be advanced or, more broadly, that different social and political 'meanings' can be articulated in rival and competitive ideological discourses is that the concepts through which these 'meanings' assume shape and form are marked by an inherent contestability. Or, to reiterate Freeden's core intuition or basic point: the concepts through which we assemble and attribute 'meaning' to social and political life are, in the famous terms of W. B. Gallie, 'essentially contestable'.[15] Two related implications necessarily follow from this suggestion. First, it becomes impossible to objectively adjudicate between the relative merits of one ideological discourse as against another, if by 'objectively adjudicate' we mean that one discourse or perspective can be shown to be grounded in the real, where the 'real' signifies certain indisputable 'facts' about the social or political. The reason for this, insists Freeden, is that supposedly descriptive 'facts' about the social or political world are inevitably mediated through concepts that are also marked by an inherent contestability.[16] Therefore, and second, the idea of a critique of ideology grounded in the real is always-already problematic to the extent that it is mediated through contestable concepts that do not merely describe the reality of the social, but, as Freeden puts it, 'create . . . the reality to which we relate'.[17]

Taken together, then, the contemporary ideology theory of Freeden and Ricoeur clearly stands against the Marxian suggestion that the real can be critically distinguished from the ideological. For whether we conceive ideology as a 'decontested ordering of the political' (Freeden) or as an assumed 'interpretative code' (Ricoeur), the inference in both cases is the same: namely, that ideology plays a constitutive role in shaping the meanings we invest in social reality. Or, to put it in a slightly different fashion, ideology needs to be understood as importantly conditioning the real, as an inescapable or omnipresent social phenomenon to the degree that it is necessarily reflected in the sense-creating activities of social actors. It is important to note that Freeden's and Ricoeur's suggestion that the real is, in effect, always-already ideological is a popular and widely held intuition among many other contemporary theorists of ideology. Indeed, it would not be an exaggeration to say that the relatively recent history of social, political and cultural theory has been increasingly marked by the refrain that it is incredibly difficult, if not impossible, to draw any clear-cut or substantive critical distinction between the real and the ideological.[18] That is to say, many would agree with Ricoeur's dictum that 'we cannot speak of a pre-ideological or non-ideological activity' – by which he means that we cannot advocate a belief in a non-ideological or pre-ideological real without paradoxically engaging in the ideological activity of interpreting and investing it with meaning.[19]

It is important that we begin to foreground the thought of Habermas, Žižek and Deleuze at this point. For Habermas, Žižek and Deleuze all insist on the intuition that a distinction can indeed be drawn between the real and the ideological. Each of these thinkers, as I said at the beginning of the introduction, offers us a critique of ideology that intuitively relies on the notion of a non-ideological or pre-ideological real. Generally speaking, then, the ideology theory of Habermas, Žižek and Deleuze has more in common with that of Marx and Engels than that of Ricoeur or Freeden, at least when it comes to thinking about how the relation between the ideological and the real is theorized. Indeed, it is worth noting in passing that Freeden is particularly and explicitly concerned to distance himself from the broader deficiencies of Marx and Marxian approaches to ideology. The 'Marxist conception of ideology', he argues,

> has . . . placed scholarly blinkers on the variegated nature of ideology by encouraging certain analytical directions and readings rather than others. It

ascribes a pejorative meaning to ideology, exposing it as a distorted or inverted reflection of alienated socially produced thought, and opposing it to true consciousness . . . It identifies a particular historically situated epistemology which gives rise to ideology, thus implying its ephemerality rather than ubiquity.[20]

Directing these remarks to Habermas, Žižek and Deleuze, we can say that their approach to ideology is, in Freeden's terms, clearly implicated to the extent that it entails a kind of Marxian insistence on the 'emphemerality rather than ubiquity' of the ideological. The critical point again being that a Marxian-inspired critique of ideology grounded in the 'real' (however conceived) fails to appreciate how forms of ideology actually give shape to the meanings we invest in social reality. In this, of course, we touch importantly on the crucial distinction between a Freeden-inspired approach to ideology and the critical conception of ideology that we will garner from Habermas, Žižek and Deleuze. The argument to be made is this: an approach such as Freeden's (Ricoeur is equally implicated here) militates against the possibility of a critique of ideology by implying that there is no critical space outside the ubiquitous influence of the ideological, no real or genuine way to make critical judgements concerning the nefarious forms of ideology we encounter in social life. I will come back to this crucial point in the concluding chapter.[21] But before I run ahead of myself here, I need to refocus on Habermas, Žižek and Deleuze, and I need, more particularly, to come to grips with how they each theorize the relation between the real and the ideological. So how, then, do Habermas, Žižek and Deleuze specifically theorize the relation between the real and the ideological? And, more generally, how do their different approaches imply and connect up with one another? We can take each question and anticipate each thinker in turn. Habermas, as we shall see, provides us with a 'communicative' or, what he also calls, 'post-metaphysical' conception of the real. By this Habermas means that social reality is necessarily and inevitably a product of the meanings that social actors invest in it, and that these meanings are bound by the form of 'communicative action' in which they engage. We will come to see how Habermas explicitly justifies this claim in the concluding part of chapter 2. For the moment, though, it is necessary to give an initial indication of the implications that this idea of the real has for Habermas's concept of ideology. The basic point is this: ideology, for Habermas, signifies a repression or truncation of the fundamentally communicative structure of the real, or, more particularly, of the social relations that are its necessary product. That is to say, ideology operates in the social world by instituting itself in a way that fails to do justice to the communicative structure of social relations. We will come to see how this intuition can be mapped out and made more concrete as chapters 2 and 3 unfold.[22]

The manner in which Žižek theorizes the distinction between the ideological and the real is markedly different from Habermas. Rather than drawing on language philosophy or communication theory to argue for a communicative conception of the real, Žižek draws primarily on the thought of Jacques Lacan to advocate, what can be called, a psychoanalytical conception of 'the Real'. As we shall see, the importance of this notion of 'the Real' to Žižek is virtually impossible to overemphasize, for it is the idea around which his theory of ideology so crucially turns. Key here is Žižek's stress on 'the Real' as that which signifies the 'antagonism', as he calls it, at the heart of all forms of ideology. By this Žižek means, among other things, that 'the Real' bears witness to the fragility and contestability of the meanings and assumptions that sustain any ideological image of social reality. In this respect, the critique of ideology, where 'critique of ideology' implies rendering contestable the meanings and assumptions at play in certain ideological images of social reality, touches 'the Real' and is inevitably conditioned by 'the Real' of 'antagonism'. Or, as Žižek most explicitly says, 'the Real' is a space or 'place' where we can wrestle free and gain some critical 'distance' from the ideological. The significance of this claim, and of Žižek's notion of 'the Real' as 'antagonism', will become only too apparent as chapters 4 and 5 develop.[23] When we turn to Deleuze in chapters 6 and 7 we will see immediately that he is, contra Žižek, much less concerned with drawing on psychoanalysis to theorize a critique of ideology. Indeed, Deleuze's theory of ideology, and his notion of the real, implies a direct and uncompromising critique of psychoanalysis. In order to underscore this point I will look to Deleuze's (and Guattari's) critical analysis of the Freudian theory of desire in their path-breaking book *Anti-Oedipus*.[24] What can be extrapolated from Deleuze and Guattari here is a concept of the real (where the 'real' signifies the productive coexistence of 'desire' and the 'social field') which is distinct from the forms of ideology that repress desire as such. Indeed, ideology, according to a Deleuzian perspective, necessarily functions through a repression of desire, operating when desire becomes a desire for repression. Here we are anticipating a core intuition or claim that will be further developed and reinforced as chapters 6 and 7 progress.[25]

Even from this rather brief and schematic discussion we can begin to appreciate how the theorizations of the real and the ideological we find in Habermas, Žižek and Deleuze will imply and connect up with one another. For whether we think of the real as mediated through the communicative relations in which we invest meaning in the social world (Habermas), or as constituted through the forms of desire that influence how we assign meaning to the social (Deleuze), or as that which signifies the 'antagonism' or contestability and fragility of the meanings that sustain our sense of the social (Žižek), we shall see that the basic gesture in each case is the same, or at least formally homologous: namely, that the notion of the real is intuitively theorized as a kind of pre-ideological site on to which ideology is then grafted. Needless to say, tying together the respective Habermasian, Žižekian and Deleuzian conceptions of the real in this broad and rather general way is hardly unproblematic. And merely to suggest that Habermas, Žižek and Deleuze intuitively share a concern to distinguish the real from the ideological is, of course, to say nothing, or very little, about whether the intuition can be justified as such. In the eighth and concluding chapter I will argue that there is a particular sense or way in which this intuition can indeed be justified or maintained, and that it can be explicitly maintained against the backcloth of the kind of ideology theory – exemplified, as we have already seen, by Ricoeur and Freeden – that insists on problematizing the possibility of drawing any clear-cut distinction between the real and the ideological.[26]

Ideology and the ethical or moral

When it comes to theorizing the relation between the ideological and the ethical or moral (here I will use the terms 'ethical' and 'moral' interchangeably), the crucial concern is to show how ideology critique necessarily proceeds on certain moral or ethical grounds.[27] The basic point to be advanced is this: the critique of ideology always proceeds on certain ethical or moral grounds to the extent that it implies a critical evaluation of values, where a 'critical evaluation of values' involves insisting on the cultivation of certain values as against others that are considered normatively deficient or ethically problematic in some way. Understood on this rather formal basis, Habermas, Žižek

INTRODUCING THE CRITICAL CONCEPTION OF IDEOLOGY 13

and Deleuze all offer a critique of ideology that is morally or ethically oriented. This crucial point will be explicitly underlined and retrospectively reinforced in the final chapter, although it will, in a sense, be anticipated in and through arguments encountered from earlier chapters. In chapter 3, for example, we shall see that Habermas insists on normative or moral values such as 'social reciprocity' and 'individual autonomy' as against the norms and values implied by, what he calls, 'consumerism', 'technocratic consciousness' or the ideological 'prejudices' of 'tradition'.[28] In chapter 5, for instance, we shall see that Žižek places great stress on, among other things, the value of 'ethical responsibility' as against, what he would call, the 'perverse' and 'instrumentalizing' ideology of 'Nazism', fascism or, more generally put, 'totalitarianism'.[29] In chapter 7, to anticipate one final example, we shall see that Deleuze emphasizes the value of a liberating or joyous desire, where this signifies the subject's struggle against that which represses it; or against that which turns desire into an ideological desire for repression.[30] It is on terms such as these that Habermas, Žižek and Deleuze could be thought to be engaging in an ethical or moral critique of ideology.

Of course, to claim that we can engage in an ethical or moral critique of ideology, that the critique of ideology is always inflected with a distinct moral or ethical sense, is hardly uncontroversial or incontestable. The reason for this is clearly that notions such as the 'ethical' or 'moral' are, in themselves, highly controversial and contested concepts, and that their meanings are undoubtedly complicated by the way they are mediated through various, and competing, discourses. From the point of view of a 'critical conception of ideology', at least as we will understand it here, this insight is an important and potentially troubling one. For an ideology theorist such as Bernard Susser, for example, the idea of a moral or ethical critique of ideology would be decidedly problematic in the sense that it implies a strict separation of the terms 'ideological', 'ethical' or 'moral'. And rather than getting involved in a 'definitional wrangle', as he would call it, about how to distinguish the 'ideological' from the 'ethical' or 'moral', it is, in his view, necessary to understand the ideological as a form of 'discourse' that may well assume a particular 'moral' or 'ethical' shape.[31] Or, by again drawing on Michael Freeden, we could push the point even further in suggesting that any sense we social actors may develop of the 'moral' or the 'ethical' is always-already 'ideological' to the extent that it is mediated through the institution of 'essentially contestable' concepts.[32]

Consider, for illustrative purposes or by way of example, the concept of 'multiculturalism'. This has become something of a buzzword in contemporary social, political and cultural life. In academic circles 'multiculturalism' has clearly assumed the status of a moral or ethical discourse, signifying a call for, among other things, a democratization of culture and a respect for 'difference' or, what is also called, the 'other'. According to Charles Taylor's famous thesis, 'multiculturalism' implies a 'politics of recognition' which must, as he puts it:

> suppose that cultures that have provided a horizon of meaning for large numbers of human beings . . . over a long period of time . . . are almost certain to have something that deserves our admiration and respect . . . Perhaps one could put it another way: it would take supreme arrogance to discount this possibility *a priori*.[33]

It is evident that Taylor wants to inflect his notion of a multicultural sensibility with a substantive moral or ethical sense, the moral or ethical gesture being that we be steadfast in our 'admiration' and 'respect' for other 'cultures' that have provided a historically significant 'horizon of meaning' for their members. Failure to adopt this multicultural sensibility is, as Taylor explicitly says, a 'moral failing', reflecting the 'supreme arrogance' of those ethnocentrically immured by their own cultural norms and values.[34] The moral or ethical discourse advocated by Taylor here can easily be reframed in our terms as a critique of ideology. For we clearly have a critical evaluation of values; that is, an insistence on the moral or ethical value of a multicultural sensibility as against the ideological seduction of one's own ethnocentrically inflated norms, values or standards. Taylor, in other words, provides us with a moral or ethical critique of ideology. Now, Freeden's point would be that we must retain a critical sensitivity to how this sense of the moral or ethical – that is, this concept of a multicultural sensibility – can be mobilized in the to and fro of ideological argument, and how it can be subject to ideological contestation. Think, for instance, about the impact of an ideology such as 'feminism', its ability to mobilize or employ an ethical discourse underpinned by a multicultural sensibility and a demand, in Taylor's terms, for 'recognition'. That is to say, the history of feminism has been marked by the way it has contested the non-recognition or ideological misrecognition of women, cautioning us to be aware of how patriarchal societies and forms of patriarchal ideology have traditionally induced women to adopt a depreciatory image of themselves, forcing them to internalize a picture of their supposed inferiority.[35] Coming back to Freeden, we could say that feminism is, like all morally inflected discourses, an 'ideological reading of ideology' precisely because it contests or challenges established or traditional ideological points of view and establishes itself as an ideological player in the social field.[36] Let us tie this back into Habermas, Žižek and Deleuze. The implication that necessarily follows from Freeden's analysis is that we must recognize a certain collapsing together of the moral, the ethical and the ideological, and that a sober analysis and critique of moral or ethical theory is only possible when we acknowledge its power as a vehicle for ideological thinking. And if, as Freeden argues, the moral or the ethical is always-already ideological, then to maintain a critical distinction between them becomes impossible. That is to say, a moral or ethical critique of ideology that supposedly, and by implication, must move beyond or transcend the ideological turns out, in truth, to be just another form of ideology. And the supposedly ideology-free or ideology-transcendent concepts employed in moral or ethical critique (for example, Habermas's notions of reciprocity and autonomy, Žižek's idea of ethical responsibility, or Deleuze's concept of a joyous and liberating desire) are, therefore, all inevitably tainted by the ideological. It is important to acknowledge that the kind of problematization of the moral, ethical and ideological we find in Freeden here would strike a chord with many other contemporary students or theorists of ideology. Ernesto Laclau, for example, would immediately censor and caution us to remain critically sensitive to, what he calls, the 'hegemonic' and, ultimately, ideological consequences that follow from theorizations of the moral or the ethical.[37] It is against the backcloth of this type of scepticism that I will ultimately seek to defend or use Habermas, Žižek and Deleuze to justify the claim that ideology critique ought to, and needs to, proceed on certain moral or ethical grounds: that is, on the grounds of a critical evaluation of values. This will be an argument that I explicitly take up in the eighth and concluding chapter.[38]

The way ahead

What I have been concerned to do thus far is to paint in rather broad brush strokes how the central themes of the book will emerge and be mapped out; to provide, where appropriate, some context as to how these themes have been taken up at different points in the history of ideology theory; and to anticipate some possible criticisms that may be levelled at the 'critical conception of ideology' that will be extrapolated from Habermas, Žižek and Deleuze. Before concluding, or by way of concluding this first or introductory chapter, I will be a little more specific about the structure of the book, or, better still, give a brief indication of the way its argument will gather momentum in subsequent chapters. In chapters 2 and 3 I will focus on Habermas, introducing the critical distinction that he wants to draw between the real and the ideological (chapter 2), before further exploring the moral or normative content of his ideology critique (chapter 3). In chapters 4 and 5 I look to Žižek, introducing his critical differentiation of 'the Real' from the ideological (chapter 4), before exploring the ethics implied by his critique of ideology (chapter 5). And in chapters 6 and 7 I consider the work of Deleuze, introducing the Deleuzian distinction between the real and the ideological (chapter 6), before exploring the ethical terms on which a Deleuze-inspired critique of ideology could proceed (chapter 7).[39] In the eighth and final chapter I will engage in a cross-comparative and critical analysis of the Habermasian, Žižekian and Deleuzian theories of ideology previously outlined. The critical gesture to be made here is to play one thinker against the other in order to problematize each respectively (such that I will mount Habermasian arguments against Deleuze, Deleuzian arguments against Žižek, Žižekian arguments against Habermas and so on).

Two important points will necessarily follow from this critical analysis. First, the moral or ethical terms on which Habermas's, Deleuze's and Žižek's respective critiques of ideology proceed will, when cross-compared, be rendered contestable and problematic. And, second, the ways in which Habermas, Deleuze and Žižek intuitively draw a critical distinction between the real and the ideological will be equally rendered contestable and problematic. Therefore, the crucial question that this discussion will raise concerns whether it is actually possible to defend the basic intuitions of a critical conception of ideology in light of such a problematization of Habermasian, Deleuzian and Žižekian thought. And, as I have already partly indicated or implied, it is this question that I will affirmatively wrestle with in the fourth and final part of chapter 8.

One final thing is worth acknowledging and anticipating by way of introduction, and it relates to my concern to use film or cinema as a backcloth against which to grapple with the theories of ideology offered to us by Habermas, Žižek and Deleuze. There will be a number of instances of this in the chapters to follow. In chapter 3, for instance, I shall draw on aspects of Gary Ross's *Pleasantville* (1998) in order to make sense of Habermas's notion of 'moral autonomy'; in chapters 4 and 5, we shall see how Žižek theorizes freedom or autonomy by way of an analysis of the actions of Keyser Soeze in Bryan Singer's *The Usual Suspects* (1995); in chapter 6, I shall draw on Deleuze's reading of Alfred Hitchcock's *Rope* (1948) in order to render more concrete his theory of subjectivity; and in chapter 7, I shall engage in a Deleuzian or Deleuze-inspired reading of Paul Thomas Anderson's *Magnolia* (1999). What motivates this use of film is not simply the assumption that the cinematic text provides a rich backcloth against which to discuss abstract, and often difficult, theory (although it can certainly do that, and I will, as indicated above, use it to that end). My use of cinema, or my engagement with films such as *Pleasantville, The Usual Suspects, Rope* and *Magnolia* is also intuitively guided by the idea – an idea that I take directly from Deleuze and Žižek in particular – that cinematic texts can do theory in their own right, that they have their own 'autonomy' to the extent that they generate ideas or concepts that can move us and force us to think differently about the social and the political.[40] From the point of view of a 'critical conception of ideology', it is important to acknowledge how a cultural or media form such as film can both reproduce and/or contest ideology; how a piece of cinema such as Paul Thomas Anderson's *Magnolia* can be seen to express a sense of the subject's experience of ideological repression as well as the desire to move critically beyond such repression.[41]

2 • Habermas's Ideology Theory

In this chapter and the next I will focus on the critical theory of Jürgen Habermas, introducing his ideology theory (chapter 2) before further exploring the explicitly normative or moral content of his ideology critique (chapter 3). Before anticipating and introducing some of the main themes and issues that will arise from this engagement with Habermas's work, it is perhaps important to point out that the particular analysis undertaken here is, in many ways, a curious one. That is to say, much of the recent secondary literature and critical commentary on Habermas rarely concerns itself with his ideology theory. This is particularly so in political studies (or in English-speaking political theory), where Habermas is often, for example, mobilized to focus more explicitly on questions of justice, or to answer the question of what justice demands in a modern, pluralistic society.[1] While this kind of critical commentary is undoubtedly important, and while Habermas's recent work in political and legal theory clearly merits such commentary and exposition, it is also crucial that we do not lose sight of the fact that Habermas's particular brand of critical theory is still intuitively guided by a clear notion of ideology critique, and by a clear conception of the ideological. In this way, my approach to Habermas's work perhaps has more in common with those adopted in sociology, in media studies, even in philosophy, particularly where stress is placed on the German or, more broadly, European tradition in which his thought is embedded.[2]

So what kind of ideology theory are we talking about here? As we anticipated in chapter 1, and as we shall see in this chapter, Habermas's thought is intuitively guided by the possibility of maintaining a critical conception of ideology, where 'critical conception of ideology' partly implies differentiating the ideological from the real. Crucial to this endeavour is the development of a 'communicative' or, what Habermas would also call, 'postmetaphysical' idea of social reality. By this Habermas means that social reality is necessarily a product of the meanings that social actors invest in it, and that these meanings are bound by the form of communicative action that they engage in. Or, put another way, the communicative nature of social reality is importantly reflected in the fact that the self-conscious meanings we invest in the social world are crucially conditioned in linguistically mediated action. I will explicitly come back to how Habermas justifies this claim in the third and concluding part of the chapter. For the moment, though, it is necessary to anticipate the implications that this notion of the real has for Habermas's concept of ideology. Put simply, ideology, for Habermas, signifies a repression or truncation of the communicative. More particularly, ideology functions or operates in the social world by instituting itself in a way that fails to do justice to the indelibly communicative structure of social relations. Again, this is a significant point that I will need to introduce at the end of the chapter. And when I do come to make this point we shall see that it is essentially a normative or, more broadly, moral one. That is to say, it will become clear that Habermas is concerned to critique ideology from a moral or normative point of view. This, as I have already intimated, is an issue that will preoccupy us in both this and the next chapter.

However, before I run ahead of myself on these matters it is imperative that I do some groundwork in order make fuller sense of how this Habermasian theory and critique of ideology is developed and justified. This is precisely what I will do in the first two parts of this chapter. In the first part of the chapter I will focus on Habermas's conception of reason or rationality, before shifting attention, in the second part, to his theory of subjectivity. The importance of these explorations is that they will introduce us to the key Habermasian concepts of the 'communicative' and 'postmetaphysical'. That is to say, we will witness how Habermas's 'communicative' and 'postmetaphysical' concepts of reason and the self imply, or relate to, a broader notion of the real, a 'real' that can be thought to be importantly non-ideological or pre-ideological. This idea of a non-ideological or pre-ideological real will be introduced in the third and final part of the chapter.

Reason and rationality

In his essay 'The unity of reason in the diversity of its voices', Habermas impressively and retrospectively casts an eye over a broad and diverse body of thought or philosophical speculation in order to clarify and illuminate the meaning of 'rationality'.[3] Now, this 'retrospective in the history of ideas', as Habermas calls it, is motivated not by a dry scholasticism, but by a desire to counter influential currents in contemporary thought that seek to condemn philosophical speculation about the status and scope of reason to the dustbin of history. These influential and contemporary critics of reason – 'contextualists' as Habermas would call them – are sceptical about the prospect of developing any comprehensive notion of reason because they do not accept that 'reason' itself has any significant meaning outside the particular context in which it is linguistically articulated.[4] The point, then, from a 'contextualist' perspective, is this: the supposedly comprehensive or universal domain of reason is rendered problematic to the extent that it is always-already mediated through a specific and contextually dependent form of discourse. As we shall see, Habermas will argue against this form of contextualism by suggesting that reason is indeed universal in scope and domain, and that the universality of reason is reflected in linguistically mediated social interaction or, what he more famously calls, 'communicative action oriented to mutual understanding'.

By suggesting that reason is, in some sense, *universal* Habermas is consciously and explicitly allying himself to a tradition of philosophical speculation or 'metaphysical thinking' that is as old as philosophy itself. Habermas negotiates his way through this tradition of 'metaphysical thinking' with great skill, teasing out a number of important currents which have animated its historical development. It will be useful to briefly draw on some of these currents, emphasizing all the while how they have helped fashion the idea that reason or rationality has a universal domain. The first of these currents of thought could be best described as a form of *objectivism* which seeks to locate reason in an 'objective order' that crucially transcends the contingent world of 'concrete events and phenomena'.[5] This kind of objectivism is found, for example, in the ancient Greek thought of Plato and his 'doctrine of Ideas'. Put simply, an 'Idea', according to the Platonic conception, is rational and universal to the extent that it transcends the contingent and transitory nature of the everyday material world and to the degree that it necessarily maintains an eternal or timeless quality and perfection. Plato's famous, and no less provocative, contention is that certain intellectually gifted individuals can, if they are given the right philosophical training, develop the capacity to use their reason in order to grasp or contemplate 'Ideas' in such a way that they can be used in the governance of human affairs.[6]

In this way, the use of human reason bears witness to the universal precisely because it apprehends or grasps an 'Idea' which is itself universal: that is, an 'Idea' that is characterized by an eternal or, what Habermas would call, 'supratemporal' perfection and necessity.[7]

The notion, already implicit in Platonism, that reason is universal through virtue of its 'necessity' is a core intuition that echoes through the tradition of 'metaphysical thinking'. In the modern era, for instance, we find Immanuel Kant insisting on the crucial importance of understanding reason's universal domain as something fundamentally 'necessary'. As a moral and political philosopher, Kant is particularly motivated by the possibility of understanding reason's universal domain as something fundamentally 'necessary' to the development of a just society. Consider, for instance, his famous argument in favour of, what he calls, the 'kingdom of ends'. In the 'kingdom of ends', Kant argues, individuals reason with one another as architects or authors of a 'law' that demands their allegiance by respecting their dignity both as autonomous beings and as a community. Now, the important point to maintain here is that this form of 'practical' reasoning, as Kant calls it, is necessary to the prospect of creating a just society precisely because it is an indispensable condition of it. In other words, the creation of a 'kingdom of ends' would not be possible without the use of reason, or, better still, without individuals who have the innate and universally shared capacity to reason together in matters of law and moral conduct.[8] In this sense, Kant locates the universal domain of reason in individuals themselves, by way of, what Habermas calls, a 'subjective faculty' for rational thought.[9] Kant, then, presents us with a form of 'metaphysical thinking' that is *subjectivist* in orientation.[10]

Hegel's 'metaphysical thinking' importantly differs from Kant's in the sense that it is clearly defined, as Habermas points out, by a *historicist* orientation.[11] Simply put, Hegel is concerned to locate the universal domain of reason in history, or, better still, in a conception of historical change and progress. Reason, from a Hegelian perspective, is not an object of philosophical training and contemplation (as in Plato), nor is it the universally shared faculty of autonomous agents (as in Kant): rather, reason *becomes* increasingly more universal in and through the process of a self-directed and progressive history. Put simply, then, history operates in accordance with a form of reason that turns out, through time, to be more and more universal in its scope and domain. Hegelian thought marks, from a Habermasian perspective, a decisive moment in the tradition of 'metaphysical thinking' precisely because it importantly paves the way for its critique and ultimate rejection.[12] Hegel's core intuition that reason is mediated through history or is *historically situated* echoes down to the present day through currents of contemporary thought that would question and remain resolutely sceptical of the Hegelian project. Hegel, according to contemporary critics, is not sensitive enough to the fact that reason is inescapably encumbered or weighed down by history or historical forms of life that bear the contingent imprint of a particular time and place.[13] In this way, the recognition of the historicity of reason leads, contra Hegel, to an inevitable questioning of the 'metaphysical' assumption that reason has a universal domain. Habermas sums up the difficulties that are brought into sharp relief by modern and contemporary forms of post-Hegelian historicism when he writes: 'it has become ever harder to ignore the way in which history intrudes into the structures of . . . reason with the contingencies of what is unforeseeably new and other, and these contingencies belie all rash . . . and limiting constructions.'[14]

Taken together, Hegelianism, Kantianism and Platonism – indeed the whole 'metaphysical tradition' as Habermas defines it – becomes increasingly problematic and questionable when viewed through the lens of historicism. The historicist wants to wrestle free from the grip of 'metaphysical thinking' precisely because s/he considers unjustified the suggestion that reason has a universal domain. In this way, historicism inextricably connects up with the 'contextualism' I spoke of earlier. The historicist-contextualist point can be made clear in the following terms: reason does not, and cannot, have a comprehensive universal domain precisely because it is always a product of a particular history, and is thereby contextually anchored in a specific form of cultural life. Habermas takes this contextualist critique of metaphysics seriously, agreeing that it is important to give due intellectual weight to the intuition that reason is mediated through historically and culturally specific contexts. Reason, as Habermas puts it, always functions in 'the here and now'.[15] Importantly, though, he also wants to reject the contextualist – or 'radical contextualist' as he sometimes calls it – argument that reason is always particular, that standards of rationality never transcend context, and that, ultimately, there can be no form or use of reason that is universal in scope and domain. Habermas, in other words, still retains an important connection to the metaphysical tradition by intuitively holding fast to the idea that reason can function in a way that moves beyond context. Reason,

Habermas says, 'transcends spaces and times'.[16] So we see that Habermas is concerned to tread a careful line between a form of metaphysical rationalism that remains insufficiently sensitive to context, and a 'radical' contextualism that rejects any possibility of developing a notion of reason that is universal in scope and domain. The treading of this careful line is the intellectual task that lies before Habermas as a self-professed *postmetaphysical thinker*.

Habermas's 'postmetaphysical thinking' on rationality turns crucially on his notion of language or, more specifically, on the emphasis he places on language as the fundamental medium through which reason is constituted. Reason, according to Habermas, is given its meaning and definitive shape through discourse or forms of 'communicative action oriented to mutual understanding'. What does this mean? When interlocutors or communicative actors come together in dialogue and debate they, according to Habermas, inevitably or invariably reason with one another by raising claims and making arguments that seek to convince others of the efficacy of their view.[17] We can say that communicative actors or interlocutors can legitimately win others around to their view only by rationally convincing them through, what Habermas calls, the sheer 'force of the better argument'. In this way, communicative action can be understood as rational to the extent that it reflects a form of reasoned agreement or consensus which is grounded in the intersubjective recognition of the 'better argument'. Now, the point that Habermas would want to make here is not that all forms of dialogue between individuals are grounded in such rational terms as a matter of brute empirical fact: rather, he is claiming that the notion of reasoned or rational agreement grounded in the better argument is itself a necessary condition of the social relations developed between communicative actors because it acts as an ideal or principle guiding their discourse together. Reason, in this way, is an ideal – or an idealizing presupposition – which nonetheless invariably or necessarily shapes and informs practical and concrete discursive exchanges.[18]

With this communicative conception of reason to hand, we can begin to see how Habermas's postmetaphysical thinking is intended to tread a careful line between metaphysical rationalism and radical contextualism. Three points follow from what has been said thus far. First, Habermas wants to insist that reason has a universal scope and domain in the sense that it is a necessary or unavoidable aspect of linguistically mediated social interaction. Yet, and second, this 'metaphysical' assumption needs to be tempered or rendered 'postmetaphysical' by the recognition that reason or reasoned discourse always contingently emerges from within the confines of a particular historical-cultural context. This, by way of a third point, does not mean that reason is irredeemably or incorrigibly imprisoned by context: rather, reasoned discourse grounded in agreement only makes sense, contends Habermas, if it is intuitively anchored by claims that are justified in, what he calls, a 'context-bursting' manner.[19] In other words, any given claim or argument that emerges from a particular form of dialogue can only be rationally accepted as the 'better argument' on the basis that it is intuitively justified, as Habermas would say, 'not merely in context', but in 'all possible contexts': that is, on universal terms.[20] So, it is with these core intuitions that Habermas stands against both metaphysical rationalism and radical contextualism. Between a form of rationalism insufficiently sensitive to context on the one hand, and a form of contextualism that rejects any notion of universality on the other, Habermas holds steadfastly to a 'Janus-faced' notion of 'communicative reason': that is, a conception of reason that claims to be both 'context-dependent' and 'context-transcendent'.[21]

It is important that we end our relatively brief discussion of Habermas's postmetaphysical or communicative conception of reason on a note of caution. Perhaps the most obvious point to make is that Habermas's avowed commitment to rationalism, or his belief that reason has a universal domain, is contentious, provocative, and, as such, has been subject to much critical commentary from his contemporaries. Indeed, we shall see in subsequent chapters how Slavoj Žižek and Gilles Deleuze develop ideas and concepts that are quite foreign to Habermas's, and which, particularly in the case of Deleuze, put a question mark against certain assumptions that are fundamental to his particular brand of rationalism.[22] For the moment, though, it is enough to rest content with an exploration of Habermas's thought 'from the inside', as it were. In particular, I will explore Habermas's concept of the person, or, more technically put, theory of subjectivity. It is necessary to immediately point out that Habermas's theory of subjectivity is animated, much like his theory of rationality or reason, by a form of 'postmetaphysical thinking' that is grounded on communicative terms. This, as we shall see presently, is another way of simply saying that Habermas provides us with a conception of the person that he considers to be resolutely postmetaphysical and indelibly communicative.

Self, other and communicative action

'Individuality', Habermas categorically states, 'forms itself in relations of intersubjective acknowledgement and . . . intersubjectively mediated self-understanding.'[23] So we immediately see that in order to develop a conception of the self or subjectivity, Habermas insists on the need to think about how the self relates to the other in language – the obvious point being that we cannot even begin to answer the question of what constitutes a self if we ignore or repress the intuition that subjectivity is given definitive shape and meaning through virtue of its linguistically mediated relationship to the other. The self, in this way, is a fundamentally communicative being. In order to make sense of this crucial intuition Habermas looks to the work of the American social psychologist George Herbert Mead. One of the main motivations driving Habermas's reconstruction of Mead's philosophy is his desire to strip the self, or concept of subjectivity, of the metaphysical trappings with which it has historically been encumbered. That is to say, we shall see that the importance of Mead's work for Habermas is that it provides an opportunity for theorizing the relation between the self and other in a way that is no longer constrained by the questionable assumptions of 'metaphysical thinking'. Mead, then, according to Habermas, needs to be acknowledged as a truly original thinker: a genuinely postmetaphysical thinker committed to teasing out the implications of, what he calls, an 'intersubjectivistic' conception of the self.

Habermas's image of a subject indelibly shaped through linguistically mediated interaction is, he argues, something quite foreign to the tradition of metaphysical thinking that has historically failed to adequately capture or intellectually grasp the intersubjective core of the self. We can see this historical failure reflected in the way metaphysical thinking reduces, constrains and, consequently, devalues the individual by treating it as a degraded or lower form of existence or 'being'.[24] In a way, the problem here is that the individual or the self is treated *too impersonally*, as a *thing* whose essence, dignity and autonomy is not reflected in itself, but in its relation to that which is supposedly more essential or dignified. Habermas is critical of this image of the self on both philosophical and political grounds. Philosophically speaking, there is a failure to acknowledge the singularity, or particularity, of the self. And this denial of the uniqueness of the person is politically regressive in the sense that it implies a certain curtailment of autonomy: that is, the autonomous right that the self has in defining its own uniqueness in relation to the other. Put somewhat colloquially, then, this form of metaphysical thinking fails to get personal enough about the self because it fails to invest enough philosophical value and importance in the autonomy or irreplaceable uniqueness inherent in the structure of subjectivity. Without such an acknowledgement of individual autonomy, Habermas argues, there can be no adequate theorization of the self's relation to the other.[25]

By implicitly relying on the idea that the self has a uniqueness and autonomy, Habermas's notion of subjectivity reconstructs a crucial intuition that is at play in a resolutely modern current of intellectual thought: 'the philosophy of consciousness' as he calls it. However, it is necessary to stress that Habermas's reconstruction of the philosophy of consciousness is intended as a critique which aims to purge it of certain residual metaphysical assumptions. In particular, Habermas is concerned to question, what he calls, the 'decisionistic' and 'possessive' individualism implied by the philosophy of consciousness.[26] Habermas's point can be summed up thus: the philosophy of consciousness implies that the autonomy and uniqueness of the self is absolutely the internal or inward possession of the individual; that the singularity of the self belongs to the individual and no one else. In a way, the problem here is that the self is treated *too personally*, as a *thing* that somehow generates its own independence and freedom in a way that is atomistically separated from all other human beings. What becomes clear here, from a Habermasian perspective, is a failure to understand or acknowledge that the autonomy, uniqueness and dignity of the self is never the exclusive property of an individual; that it is never the product of an ego-centred decision; that subjective identity always-already bears witness to an intersubjective core invariably formed out of symbolically mediated interaction. Or, as Habermas puts it:

> Because others attribute accountability to me, I gradually make myself into the one who I have become in living together with others. The ego, which seems to me to be given in my self-consciousness as what is purely my own, cannot be maintained by me solely through my own power, as it were for me alone – it does not 'belong' to me. Rather, this ego always retains an intersubjective core because the process of individuation from which it emerges runs through the network of linguistically mediated interactions.[27]

The message, then, is clear: the individual becomes who it is, becomes individuated as it were, only through the recognition of others intersubjectively encountered in linguistically mediated interactions. This, Habermas never tires of saying, is the great lesson of Mead's philosophy; and Mead needs to be acknowledged as one of the first to have really thought through the implications of this intersubjective model of the self. Of course, this is not to imply that the 'intersubjectivistic' or postmetaphysical notion of the self is beyond critical reproach; being free, we might say, from all tensions and possible difficulties. One, perhaps obvious, difficulty or tension concerns how we are to theorize the autonomy of the individual in relation to a potentially over-determining, even repressive, communal and communicative context. The obvious worry or concern here is that the autonomy of the individual is in danger of being severely truncated if it is not given its full freedom to stand independently of the community in which it finds itself. Habermas would categorically reject such criticism, emphasizing constantly how individual autonomy and, what he calls, 'the communication community' through which it is mediated are essentially two sides of the same coin.[28] From a Habermasian perspective, everything hinges on the possibility of theorizing the relation between the self (as autonomous individual) and the other (as 'communication community') as mutually presupposing and equi-primordial. Simply put, there can be no individuation without socialization through symbolically mediated interaction; and, simultaneously, there can be no 'communication community' without the interventions of individuals who autonomously invest meaning and value in their shared social world. In trying to illuminate this fundamental intuition, this inextricable 'interlacing of individuation and socialization' as he calls it, Habermas draws explicitly on Mead by quoting a passage from the latter's 'The Genesis of the Self and Social Control':

> each individual slices the events of community life that are common to all from a different angle from that of any other individual . . . each individual stratifies the common life in a different manner, and the life of the community is the sum of these stratifications . . .[29]

The point that Habermas extrapolates from this is that the individuality of the individual is always ensured in a 'communication community' where claims to be recognized as a 'unique and irreplaceable' self are guaranteed as an unavoidable condition of linguistically mediated interaction. Simply put, communicative action between interlocutors would be impossible to sustain without the presupposition that all the actors party to the dialogical exchange are reciprocally recognized as having an individual right to assert their autonomy in the first person. Habermas refers to this as a 'moment of idealization' which is immanent to each and every communicative exchange as such.[30] Further, Habermas would suggest that this universal guarantee of individual autonomy in symbolically mediated interaction paves the way for practical change, renewal and innovation with the communication community itself. Think, for example, about how an individual or a group may, in the course of grappling with a difficult moral or ethical problem, come to the conclusion that the norms, codes and conventions that inhere within their communication community fail to do justice to their considered point of view. In this context, the individual or group is, Habermas would say, 'thrown back' on itself to the degree that it autonomously stands against the conventional morality of the community.[31] Now, in order to substantiate or render concrete this critique of conventional morality, individual communicative actors must re-engage with their fellow interlocutors in order to project a somewhat different or renewed form of morality that, if acceptable to others, would consequently give a different normative or moral shape to the communication community. In sum, the possibility of reconstructing the norms and values of the communication community is something that is ensured by its own 'unconditional' and non-negotiable respect and recognition of individual autonomy.[32]

The real and the ideological

So what, the reader may be forgiven for asking, do these ruminations have to do with the concept of ideology? The crucial issue here, as indicated in the introductory part of the chapter, is whether there is implied within Habermas's 'postmetaphysical' or 'communicative' thinking a broader notion of the real that can be distinguished from ideology. To anticipate again an argument or claim that is yet to be fully made, we could say that Habermas does indeed provide us with a way to think through the critical differentiation of the real from the ideological. Let me try to make fuller or better sense of this suggestion. Three related moves are necessary in this context. First, and perhaps most obviously, we need explicitly to underline or reinforce the idea that Habermas offers us a communicative conception of social reality.

Second, we need to explore the terms on which Habermas justifies this commitment to a communicative conception of social reality. And third, we need to begin to think about how a distinction between the real and the ideological can be maintained by drawing on the communicative conception of social reality. These, then, are the related themes that will animate the discussion in this final part of the chapter.

In what sense, then, does Habermas offer us a communicative conception of social reality? As I suggested at the beginning of the chapter, the basic Habermasian point is this: the real or social reality is necessarily a product of the meanings that social actors invest in it, and these meanings are bound by the form of communicative action that they engage in. Or, put another way, the communicative nature of social reality is importantly reflected in the fact that the self-conscious meanings we invest in the social world are crucially conditioned in linguistically mediated action. I will have an opportunity to again come back to this crucial claim or intuition in the next chapter.[33] For the moment, though, it is important to acknowledge that this image of a communicative or postmetaphysical 'real' was, in a way, always-already implied by the Habermasian notions of reason and subjectivity discussed in the previous two parts of the chapter. We can briefly take each concept in turn. As we have seen, Habermas provides us with a thoroughly communicative conception of rationality by emphasizing how reason is given its definitive shape and meaning through discourse or dialogue. Further still, we saw how Habermas argued for the universality and constitutive power of reason by claiming that the norm or ideal supposition of reasoned agreement – that is, the notion of a consensus grounded in the intersubjective recognition of the 'better argument' – is itself a necessary condition of the social relations developed between dialogical actors. Now, if this argument intuitively presupposes a communicative conception of the real, then this is clearly because communicative action or linguistically mediated interaction itself is implicitly theorized as that which necessarily conditions how we invest meaning in our intersubjectively shared world. Communicative action, to put it another way, conditions the real or, better still, is indelibly part of any sense of the 'real' that we can develop as social and linguistically mediated beings.[34] This brings us inevitably to Habermas's theory of subjectivity or notion of the self, the simple point here being that any sense of the 'real' we may develop as meaning-creating subjects is also indelibly communicative to the extent that we are all communicative beings in the first instance. As we have seen,

Habermas insists that our self of sense, and our ability to invest any coherent meaning in the world, is immediately structured in accordance with linguistically mediated interaction. Put straightforwardly, there can be no meaning invested in the 'real' without social actors who are always-already 'individuated' in and through communicative action as such.[35]

Let us now turn to the question of how precisely Habermas would justify his commitment to this communicative conception of the real, or how he would rationalize this particular image of social reality. Philosophically speaking, Habermas's commitment to a communicative conception of social reality is as strong and as substantive as it could be. That is to say, Habermas is committed to the idea that social reality is *transcendentally* conditioned by communicative action, as the latter is taken to operate as an indispensable or, as Habermas would say, 'unavoidable' feature of the former.[36] Now, the significance of this transcendental commitment to a communicative conception of social reality is reflected in the fact that Habermas uses it as the basis for his critical and normative social theory. By drawing on a strong claim concerning the fundamentally communicative nature of the social world, Habermas is able to engage in a critique of what he considers to be the morally problematic, or normatively deficient, pathologies of modern political or public life. In order to make this move from a theory of communicative action to normatively grounded social-political critique, Habermas clearly needs to establish their linkage or relationship. And this is precisely what he does by emphasizing that communicative action itself always-already has a strictly normative content or aspect, and that this normativity can be used as a critical standard against which to judge and critique the pathologies of modern political life. Before giving an example of what Habermas considers to be a pathology of modernity – and this, we shall see below, will prove useful in developing an understanding of the Habermasian theory of ideology – it is necessary that we begin to clarify the sense in which communicative action has a normative content or moral aspect. In a rather obvious sense, communicative action has a normative aspect because it is governed by norms that have a distinctively moral resonance and purpose. What kind of moral norms does Habermas have in mind here? Consider the following set of remarks:

> Whoever enters into discussion with the serious intention of becoming convinced of something through dialogue with others has to . . . assume . . .

a speech situation that satisfies improbable conditions: . . . inclusiveness, equal rights to participation, immunization against external . . . compulsion, as well as the participant's orientation toward reaching understanding (that is, the sincere expression of utterances).[37]

A number of points are worthy of our attention in light of this passage. Most immediately, we see that communicative action, the process of entering into discussion and dialogue with others, presupposes that speech actors adopt a number of moral, or at least normatively constraining, assumptions. Extrapolating slightly, we could refer to these moral norms or constraints as follows: a) that no relevant contribution made by speech actors in communicative action may be excluded or ignored by others (that is, the condition of 'inclusiveness'); b) that communicative action must remain sufficiently open for all participants to freely select and employ speech acts in an autonomous fashion (that is, the condition of 'equal rights to participation'); c) that communicative action must remain unencumbered by extra-discursive constraints such as violence, threats, privilege etc. (that is, the condition ensuring 'immunization against external compulsion'); and d) that communicative action between interlocutors be motivated by the prospect of reaching intersubjective understanding (that is, the condition ensuring 'the sincere expression of utterances'). Again, it is imperative that we underline the *transcendental* weight that Habermas tries to lend to this argument. For these moral norms or normative conditions are, Habermas insists after a certain Kantian fashion, best thought of as necessary or 'unavoidable presuppositions' that make communicative action or discourse with others possible in the first instance.[38]

So, if we were to accept Habermas's claim that communicative action is normatively conditioned, and that this normativity is an unavoidable or transcendental feature of the communicatively mediated process through which interlocutors invest meaning in social reality, then we could rest content with the assumption that moral norms play a significant and potentially progressive role in social life. In a sense, of course, this is quite a lot to ask, especially as the very concepts of the 'normative' and the 'transcendental' are, as both Deleuze and Žižek would remind us, far from unproblematic.[39] That said, it is enough, at least for now, to assume simply that Habermas's position is consistent, as this will help us focus on an issue that is even more pressing: namely, the Habermasian theory of ideology. In simple terms, Habermas's normativism, his commitment to the idea that the meanings we invest in social reality are normatively conditioned, is employed as a critical standard against which to judge ideology. Ideology, from a Habermasian perspective, can only effectively function or operate by repressing normativity; that is, by superimposing itself on social reality in a way that fails to take due regard of the communicative and normative structure of social relations. As was implied above, a good way of illustrating this crucial point, of rendering the Habermasian notion of ideology more concrete, is to animate it through a discussion of a particularly dominant pathology of modern political life: what we can call the pathology of consumerist ideology. Let me tease this out in a little more detail.

Habermas's belief that consumerism – or, more broadly, the structuring of social relations in accordance with the imperatives of advanced capitalism – has had a negative and debilitating effect on modern public life is a conviction that he has maintained throughout his intellectual career. In *The Structural Transformation of the Public Sphere*, one of his earliest works, Habermas provides both an empirical and theoretical analysis of the influence of consumerism in the modern public realm. That is to say, he emphasizes how public institutions such as the modern press – 'the public sphere's pre-eminent institution' as he calls it – are constantly subject to commercial pressures, becoming, as it were, a mere vehicle for the consumption of 'advertising'.[40] As a critic of this developing consumerist ideology, Habermas is concerned to bring out the disparity or contradiction between the terms on which it is justified and the actual consequences of its operation. Drawing on Habermas, we could suggest that there is a disparity or contradiction between the 'idea' of consumerism and its 'ideology'. Generally speaking, the justification of the 'idea' of consumerism rests on a normatively inflected and democratic claim concerning its responsiveness to the wants and needs of the individuals who make up the public sphere. From a Habermasian perspective, though, this claim is inherently problematic, normatively deficient or ideological.[41] The essence of Habermas's critique can be summed up thus: a public sphere governed by the dictates of consumerism is, in effect, a sham and ideologically circumscribed public sphere because it operates in ways that stunt or repress democratic or, what he calls, 'rational-critical' debate on shared matters of public and political importance. It is in this sense, therefore, that we can begin to think of consumerist ideology as a pathology or disease of modern political life.[42]

Understood thus, consumerist ideology manifests two related symptoms that are worthy of our attention: atomism and apathy. In a consumer society, debate and democratic conversation in the public sphere becomes increasingly difficult precisely because the forms of 'public communication' that it facilitates are primarily directed at an atomized addressee. The 'web' of public communication, as Habermas puts it, 'becomes unravelled into acts of individuated reception'.[43] What Habermas means to say here is that mass consumption of cultural products and public information – for instance, the consumption of newspapers, television, film, books, radio – becomes so privatized and atomized that members of the modern public sphere find it practically impossible to engage in a democratic conversation with one another concerning shared matters of public importance. Further, we could say that the institutions through which public communication is mediated – the modern mass media – help to create this privatized consumptive world or 'realm of intimacy', as Habermas calls it, which leads, in his view, to increased apathy among members of the polity. That is to say, the individual of consumer society – atomized and ensconced in a privatized consumptive world – will tend, from a Habermasian perspective, to be disengaged from institutions of political and public authority, observing them only from a cynical, and thereby uncritical, distance. Again, this radically curtails the possibility of individuals collectively engaging in 'rational-critical debate' concerning issues that are of public and political significance.[44]

What this brief discussion of Habermas's critique of consumerism hopefully brings into sharper focus is the important extent to which the Habermasian theory of ideology is normative in scope and orientation. For we see that consumerism is exposed as ideological to the extent that it is revealed as normatively deficient or limited. That is to say, consumerist ideology is criticized because it fosters the kind of apathy or atomism that precludes the essentially normative pursuit of entering into 'rational-critical debate' on matters of public importance. Further, we could think, as Habermas does, of consumerism as ideologically contradictory precisely because it betrays the very normative justification that is used to sustain it. For if, as I said above, the justification of consumerism as an 'idea' rests on an essentially normative and democratic claim concerning its responsiveness to the individuals who make up the public sphere, then its 'ideological' function is reflected in the fact that it is, in the Habermasian view, an enemy of democracy, or, at the very least, an atomistic or apathetic thorn in the side of democratic conversation. Thus, we can see that the Habermasian critique of consumerist ideology is a *normative critique* first and foremost. And, it is important to note that the general significance of this point extends well beyond the particularities of the critique of consumerist ideology developed in *The Structural Transformation of the Public Sphere*. For, as I shall further discuss in the next chapter, Habermas's critique of ideology is best thought of as a normative or moral critique, or as primarily concerned to expose the ideological as that which represses the normative and communicative structure of social relations.

Let me now sum up by clarifying as clearly as possible the Habermasian distinction between the real and the ideological that is beginning to emerge from his communicative conception of social reality. The crucial point to bring into view, from a Habermasian perspective, is this: the ideological is parasitic on the real through which it is invariably conditioned. This amounts to arguing, with Habermas, that we can only make sense of the functioning of ideology by understanding it against the communicatively and normatively structured social reality or social relations through which it is transcendentally conditioned.[45] Indeed, it is perhaps best to think of this Habermasian image of communicatively and normatively structured social relations in terms of a non-ideological or, better still, pre-ideological real, where the 'real' is understood to be the communicative-normative conditions in which ideology inevitably operates. So we see, ultimately, that the Habermasian distinction between the real and the ideological is expressed in philosophically substantive terms; the former being thought of in terms of a transcendental necessity that is qualitatively different or autonomous from the mere contingent and parasitic functioning of the latter. Of course, this qualitative and substantive distinction is predicated on the assumption that the communicative and normative conditions of social reality referred to by Habermas do indeed have the transcendental status that he attributes to them. And this, I hardly need add, is far from an unproblematic assumption. As I have already indicated or implied, Habermas's concepts of the 'normative' and the 'transcendental' can be rendered problematic when viewed through the lens of Deleuzian and Žižekian theory. These are issues that I will directly or explicitly address in the eighth and concluding chapter. But before I can give due consideration to a potential Žižekian or Deleuzian critique of Habermas's 'transcendentalism' or 'normativism', it will prove useful to develop a fuller and more concrete sense of the

Habermasian theory of ideology that I have begun to introduce here. More particularly, it is necessary to underscore further the importance that the concept of the normative or the moral plays in Habermas's critical theory, and specifically in his ideology critique. And this is precisely what I will do in the next chapter.

3 • Habermas's Moral Critique of Ideology

As we saw in chapter 2, Habermas's critique of ideology, and his theory of ideology more generally, is clearly normative in scope and orientation. That is to say, Habermas is concerned to critique ideology on the grounds that it is normatively deficient or morally problematic. Put simply, and somewhat more broadly, Habermas offers us a moral critique of ideology or, what is in our terms, a 'critical conception of ideology' that is inflected with a clear moral sense. The aim of this chapter will be to further explore or underscore this crucial intuition. In the first part of the chapter I will focus on Habermas's well-known argument in favour of the priority of communicative action. Or, more specifically, I will give consideration to his claim that 'communicative action oriented to mutual understanding' is, as he says, 'the original mode of language use'. The overriding significance of this argument – at least for my purposes – is that it reinforces the notion that Habermas is transcendentally committed to the idea that communicative action is decidedly moral in content or aspect. More particularly, we shall see that there is, according to Habermas, a form of social reciprocity and individual autonomy transcendentally built into the very fabric of symbolically mediated interaction. From this brief discussion of the moral significance of communicative action I move, in the second part of the chapter, to Habermas's ideology critique of 'scientism' and 'technology'. Again, the important thing to bear in mind is the moral or normative grounds on which this ideology critique is justified. Indeed, it will become clear that the Habermasian critique of technology or, what he also calls, 'technocratic consciousness' is intuitively guided by a respect for 'moral autonomy' or 'ethical freedom', the exercise of which is crucial if we harbour any ambition to critique the forms of ideology that pervade social life. It is to a discussion of this notion of moral autonomy that I turn in the third and final part of the chapter.

Communicative action and its priority

In the first volume of his *The Theory of Communicative Action* Habermas is concerned to leave his readers in no doubt of the fact 'that the use of language with an orientation to reaching understanding is the original mode of language use, upon which indirect understanding . . . and the instrumental use of language in general, are parasitic'.[1] In order to maintain the qualitative distinction between communicative action oriented to reaching understanding and the 'instrumental use of language' Habermas draws on, and reconstructs, John Austin's well-known differentiation of 'illocutionary' and 'perlocutionary' speech acts. 'Through illocutionary acts', Habermas says following Austin, 'the speaker performs an action in saying something.' The significance of illocutionary acts, for Habermas, is their 'self-sufficiency'; that is to say, 'the speech act is to be understood in the sense that the communicative intent of the speaker and illocutionary aim he is pursuing follow from the manifest meaning of what is said'.[2] In this way, speech actors pursue illocutionary aims when they engage in a form of communicative action that is transparently or manifestly oriented to understanding. In other words, the 'communicative intent' expressed is to perform a speech act 'so that a hearer may understand and accept' the validity of the utterance articulated.[3] Perlocutionary speech acts function to bring about 'effects' on the hearer. 'These effects', says Habermas, 'ensue whenever a speaker acts with an orientation to success and thereby instrumentalizes speech acts for purposes that are only contingently related to the meaning of what is said.'[4] It is important to be clear that Habermas is not just saying that speech acts can produce side effects in ways an actor cannot foresee. This 'trivial', as Habermas calls it, characterization of perlocutionary speech acts must be supplemented by a more substantive acknowledgement of how they can be formulated with the 'design', 'intention' or 'purpose' of producing consequential effects on an addressee or audience. In this way, the 'communicative intent' expressed is to perform a speech act that is strategic or, what Habermas also calls, 'teleological' in orientation.[5]

How, then, does Habermas use Austin's pragmatics in the service of his claim that communicative action oriented to mutual understanding is fundamental and prior to the 'strategic' or 'instrumental use of language'? Habermas's suggestion is that any attempt to engage in strategic action, any willing of perlocutionary effects, always-already finds itself pursuing illocutionary aims. All strategic or instrumentalizing action, in other words, must implicitly be formulated with a prior attitude to necessary understanding. This is the priority of communicative action; this is why Habermas considers it the 'original mode of language use'. He writes:

> If the hearer failed to understand what the speaker was saying, a strategically acting speaker would not be able to bring the hearer, by means of communicative acts, to behave in the desired way. To this extent . . . 'language with an orientation to consequences' is not an original use of language but the subsumption of speech acts that serve illocutionary aims under conditions of action oriented to success.[6]

Of course we may want to ask Habermas the following question: are there any circumstances in which the illocutionary aims served in a speech act are manifestly and explicitly oriented to success rather than understanding? It is necessary to point out that Habermas realizes, or has come to realize,[7] that imperatives such as: 'Pass the salt!' 'Eat your food!' and 'Close the window!' are instances where a speaker renders explicit or makes manifest a demand that is willed simply to be obeyed. In the knowledge of this, Habermas suggests that illocutionary speech acts constitute 'communicative action' only in so far as they raise 'criticizable validity claims'. Imperatives do not raise such claims: they are demanding impositions pure and simple. Habermas argues:

> Not all illocutionary acts are constitutive for communicative action, but only those with which speakers connect criticizable validity claims. In the other cases . . . when a speaker is pursuing illocutionary aims on which hearers cannot take a grounded position – as in relation to imperatives – the potential for the binding (or bonding) force of good reasons – a potential which is always contained in linguistic communication – remains unexploited.[8]

From this we can begin to appreciate the moral significance of Habermas's argument in favour of the priority of communicative action oriented to mutual understanding. Put all too simply or unproblematically,[9] communicative action ensures that social relations have a certain moral aspect or, as Habermas would say, 'normative content'. This is because communicative action, if oriented to understanding, ensures social reciprocity among speech actors, each of whom is entitled to critique and question the claims laid on them by others. That is to say, when Habermas speaks, as he does in the above passage, of the possibility of communicative actors taking a 'grounded position' in relation to claims put to them by others, he means to suggest that they have the right to adopt, what he calls, 'rationally motivated "yes" or "no" positions on the utterances of speakers'.[10] In another sense, of course, the existence of such reciprocity is also the measure of each and every speech actor's freedom; where 'freedom' signifies that all actors party to the dialogical exchange are equally recognized as having an individual right to assert their autonomy in the first person. Habermas refers to this universal and moral guarantee of reciprocity and individual autonomy as a 'moment of idealization' immanently at play in each and every communicative exchange as such.[11] So we should realize that Habermas is not simply advocating that we should, as speech actors, adopt and respect the norms of reciprocity and individual autonomy. Rather, he is suggesting that this is something we always-already do if we are concerned to engage in communicative action at all. This means that the normative or moral content of communicative action is *transcendentally* built into the very fabric or structure of symbolically mediated social interaction. And, consequently, this means that Habermas would not concede as valid the often-made criticism that he is unrealistically or idealistically asking speech or social actors to restrain their egoism in the pursuit of 'mutual understanding'. Habermas is worth quoting at length on this important point:

> Everyday praxis oriented toward understanding is permeated with unavoidable idealizations. These simply inhere in the medium of the everyday language in which the reproduction of our lives takes place. Of course, as individuals we can at any time decide to manipulate others, or to act in an openly strategic manner. But in fact not everyone could behave in this way at any time. Otherwise, for example, the category of lying would become meaningless; the grammatics of our language would in the end have to collapse. Things like the appropriation of tradition or socialization would become impossible . . . My point is that my references to idealizations have nothing to do with the ideals that the solitary theorist sets up *in opposition* to reality; I am referring only to the normative contents that are *encountered* in practice, which we cannot do without, since language, together with the idealizations it demands of speakers, is simply constitutive for sociocultural forms of life.[12]

What we are again encountering here, perhaps more concretely, is the communicative conception of the real that was introduced at the end of the last chapter. The Habermasian message, then, to repeat, is simply this: in order to invest meaning in the real or in our shared social reality, we, speech actors, need to engage in a form of communicative action oriented to mutual understanding. Clearly, the symmetrical reciprocity and respect for individual autonomy transcendentally built into this form of communicative action can be violated, or subject to strategic manipulation. However, and to state Habermas's core argument, such 'strategic action' is 'parasitic' on the essentially normative structure of communicative action on to which it is then later grafted or superimposed. This, neatly, brings us back to the issue of ideology. For 'strategic action' or the 'instrumental use of language' can be regarded as decidedly ideological to the extent that it truncates or represses the normative and communicative structure of social relations. One of the ways in which to analyse the status of strategic action, and more particularly its ideological function, is to think about it in terms of the issuing of 'imperatives'.[13] Habermas understands the function of imperatives as demanding impositions that are non-negotiable, and which circumvent communicative action. When, to use a favoured example of Habermas's, a bank robber thrusts a gun in a bank-teller's face and says 'Hands up!' he is not engaged in communicative action, but is simply issuing a demand. In this context, the normative content or, what Habermas also calls, the 'conditions of normative validity' at play in communicative action are simply repressed or replaced by the threat of sanction and the naked exercise of power.[14] Of course, the functioning or ideological operation of imperatives in social life need not simply be reduced to an individual assertion of power. Imperatives can also find their broader ideological expression in a social-institutional setting, or in more systematic terms. Indeed, it is to Habermas's credit that he is concerned to critically analyse ideological imperatives at a societal level, and in a systematic way. A good example of this is his ideology critique of, what he calls, 'technology' and 'scientism'.

Technology, scientism and ideology

The concern to critique what he considers to be the worst excesses of scientism and technology in social life is a central and enduring theme in Habermas's work. From early books such as *Toward a Rational Society* and *Theory and Practice*, to his most recent ruminations in *The Future of Human Nature*, Habermas has consistently focused on the ideological role or function that technology and scientism play in the modern public sphere. In what sense, then, are scientism and technology ideological for Habermas? Or, more immediately, what do the terms 'technology' and 'scientism' signify from a Habermasian perspective? It is perhaps best to think of Habermas's analysis of technology and scientism against the broader backcloth of his critique of positivism, where 'positivism' refers to the idea that we can technically apply scientific methods to the study of the social world.[15] Understood in this positivistic way, scientism (as a technological or technocratic ethos, as a methodological predilection, or as a body of ideas) has a long and distinguished history in social and political thinking. In the seventeenth century, for instance, we find Thomas Hobbes essentially arguing for a science of politics in which human behaviour is technically set up as a legitimate object of scientific explanation.[16] And, in a way, this Hobbesian image of a science of politics echoes through to the present day in the activities of social scientists who continue to adopt what they consider to be scientific models in their analyses of social and political life.[17] Habermas would refer to this as part of 'the scientization of politics'; a tendency that he considers crucial to the development of the modern polity. Of course, and as we have already intimated, Habermas wants to insist that this is an unwelcome or lamentable development: that the scientization of politics and the corresponding development of, what he calls, 'technocratic consciousness' is as ideological as it is morally vacuous. He is worth quoting at length here:

> Technocratic consciousness reflects . . . the repression of 'ethics' as such as a category of life . . . [It] . . . renders inert the frame of reference of interaction in ordinary language, in which domination and ideology both arise under conditions of distorted communication and can be reflectively detected and broken down. The depoliticization of the mass of the population . . . is legitimated through technocratic consciousness . . . The reified models of the sciences migrate into the sociocultural lifeworld and gain objective power of the latter's self-understanding. The ideological nucleus of this consciousness *is the elimination of the distinction between the practical and the technical* . . . [This] . . . ideology consequently violates an interest grounded in one of the . . . fundamental conditions of our cultural existence: in language, or more precisely, in the form of socialization

and individuation determined by communication in ordinary language. This interest extends to the maintenance of the intersubjectivity of mutual understanding as well as to the creation of communication without domination. Technocratic consciousness makes this practical interest disappear behind the interest in the expansion of our power of technical control.[18]

From this we can see that 'technocratic consciousness' is instantly deemed 'ideological' to the extent that it 'represses' the normative. And a key aspect of this repression of the normative is, as Habermas argues, the 'elimination of the distinction between the practical and the technical'. What Habermas means to say here is that 'technocratic consciousness' effectively precludes the raising of practical or normatively oriented questions from public discussion by turning them into purely technical questions. Think, for example, of Habermas's critique of consumerism that was discussed in chapter 2. Remember, for Habermas, that a public sphere governed by the dictates or imperatives of consumerism is a sham and ideologically circumscribed public sphere because it fosters the kind of atomism and apathy that are inimical to the development of democratic and 'rational-critical debate' on matters of public importance. In a sense, the ideological influence of consumerism or, more broadly put, economic power in social life gives shape to the formation of a certain type of 'technocratic consciousness', or a form of technocratic rationality that is purely concerned with the technical question of how to make money, maximize profit, or be efficient. Consider, for instance, the commercial dictates or economic imperatives at play in the modern press. There is, from a Habermasian perspective, an ideological tension or contradiction in the modern press to the extent that it is guided by a 'practical interest' – that is, in acting as a 'fourth estate' in democratically holding government to account, in providing citizens with impartial information on matters of public or political importance – which has been increasingly suppressed in order to meet the specific 'technical' requirements of their powerful paymasters: namely, the advertising industry.[19]

Habermas's ideology critique of technocratic consciousness clearly shows us that he is concerned to expose it on moral grounds, or in relation to its normative deficiencies. In the terms we have been using, we can say that technocratic consciousness represses the normative and communicative structure of social relations; that it functions as an 'imperative' that is non-negotiable and never subject to debate or critical questioning. This much, hopefully, is already beginning to become clear. Although the point can be made even clearer, developed and animated in more concrete terms, if we spend a little time focusing on Habermas's very recent work on the complex moral issues that are raised by new developments in biotechnology and genetic research: that is to say, if we give due consideration to his thought-provoking book *The Future of Human Nature*.[20] In this work, Habermas's concerns about the moral vacuity or bankruptcy of technocratic consciousness are again given clear articulation, not to mention a contemporary urgency. In particular, Habermas is worried by the fact that recent developments in biotechnology and genetic research force us to grapple with the notion that the human species may be able to take biological evolution into its own hands. The prospect of such a 'technological control of human nature', as Habermas puts it, gives rise to new and difficult moral questions. He frames the problem or issue in the following terms:

> The advance of the biological sciences and development of biotechnologies . . . do not just expand familiar possibilities of action, they enable a new type of intervention. What hitherto was 'given' as organic nature, and could at most be 'bred', now shifts to the realm of artifacts and their production. To the degree that even the human organism is drawn into this sphere of intervention . . . the boundary between the nature we 'are' and the organic endowments we 'give' to ourselves disappears. As a result, a new kind of self-transformation, one that reaches into the depth of the organic substrate, emerges for the intervening subject. The self-understanding of this subject now determines how one wants to use the opportunities opened up with this new scope for decision – to proceed *autonomously* according to the standards governing the normative deliberations that enter into democratic will formation, or to proceed *arbitrarily* according to subjective preferences whose satisfaction depends on the market?[21]

The question posed by Habermas at the end of this passage is self-evidently rhetorical, serving to clearly anticipate the tenor of his critique. In other words, Habermas has no desire to hide his distaste for the suggestion that individuals should be free to subjectively dispose of opportunities opened up by developing biotechnologies. This, on his view, is morally problematic. Why? Habermas asks us to think about the situation in which a parent or parents are given the opportunity to institute certain supposedly desirable genetic modifications with respect to their offspring and descendants (that is, gender, eye colour, height etc.). Now, 'as soon as adults treat the desirable traits of their descendants as a product they can shape according to a design of their own liking', Habermas says, 'they are exercising a kind of control over their genetically manipulated offspring that intervenes in . . . [their] freedom.' 'This kind of intervention', he continues, 'should be exercised over things, not persons.'[22] So we see that Habermas regards the genetic manipulation of the others' physical or natural endowments as a purely instrumental or instrumentalizing denial of their autonomy. Reduced to a 'thing' to be technically or technologically manipulated, the other person is robbed of freedom. The reason for this, argues Habermas, is that the genetically manipulated person has been immediately subjected to an irreversible and non-negotiable decision over which they can exercise no control. There is no debate, no communicative relationship or exchange, no practical deliberation or questioning, no critique, no give or take in argument. All we have are the 'imperatives' (that is, genetic traits) that follow from a specific technical or technological manipulation. This offends

> our moral sensibility because it constitutes a foreign body in the legally institutionalized relations of recognition in modern societies. When one person makes an irreversible decision that deeply intervenes in another's organic disposition, the fundamental symmetry of responsibility that exists among free and equal persons is restricted.[23]

So we see that the act of imperatively deciding to manipulate the biology of the other, the intervening in 'another's organic disposition', is signalled out by Habermas as morally insensitive, and as a particular threat of which we must be aware. And we see that this moral threat, or violation of our normative intuitions, is couched in terms of a sanction on individual freedom or autonomy. It is important that we say a little bit more about the notion of freedom or autonomy that Habermas is evoking in this context. Habermas here relies on the moral philosophy of Kierkegaard to develop his notion of the morally autonomous subject or, what he unapologetically calls, 'ethical freedom'. From a Habermasian perspective, Kierkegaard is an important thinker because he offers us the possibility of a postmetaphysical ethics, where 'postmetaphysical ethics' allows us to characterize, what he calls, 'a not-unsuccessful life'.[24] By this Habermas means that

Kierkegaard provides us with an image of what is an ethically or morally worthwhile life: a life that is not misspent, a life that is meaningful and of consequence. He refers to this as a Kierkegaardian ethic of 'being-able-to-be-oneself'. More particularly, by drawing on one of Kierkegaard's most famous works, *Either/Or*, Habermas describes the development of this ethic in the following terms:

> I *gather* myself and detach myself from the dependencies of an overwhelming environment, jolting myself to the awareness of my individuality and freedom. Once I am emancipated from a self-induced objectification, I also gain distance from myself as an individual. I pull myself out from the anonymous, scattered life that is breathlessly disintegrating into fragments and give my life continuity and transparency. In the social dimension, such a person can assume responsibility for his or her own actions and enter into binding commitments with others. In the temporal dimension, concern for oneself makes one conscious of the historicity of an existence that is realized in the simultaneously interpenetrating horizons of future and past.[25]

There is much implied by, and much to detain us, in this Kierkegaardian-inspired image of moral autonomy. But before fleshing it out in further detail, as I will do in the next part of the chapter, it is important that I make two rather more general points. First, there is a strong desire on Habermas's part to give the Kierkegaardian ethic of 'being-able-to-be-oneself' a decidedly Kantian twist; thus reflecting the profound and continuing debt his moral theory owes to Kant.[26] Following Kant, Habermas is concerned to emphasize the appeal of individual freedom on a 'formalist' basis. That is to say, the ethic of 'being-able-to-be-oneself' refers not simply to the specific ethical content of individual action, or the given ethical orientation of an individual in social-historical context. Rather, the ethic of 'being-able-to-be-oneself' transcends, as Habermas would say, the norms and values of a particular form of 'ethical life' because it refers to a mode of being or existence that has a universal and, properly speaking, 'moral' significance: that is, it can be formally applied in order to critically evaluate actions across contexts, or in any particular context.[27] So how, then, does Habermas envisage the process whereby we develop a sense of this kind of moral autonomy? Unsurprisingly, Habermas invokes his core idea of a communicative and intersubjective conception of the self to underscore the suggestion that it is only possible to understand one's own moral worth or moral autonomy in the give and take of dialogue. Put simply, and this is my second point: it is only by participating in intersubjectively shared communicative practices that we can come to any judgement about what constitutes a morally worthwhile life.[28]

Moral autonomy and ideology

Although undoubtedly formalist in tendency and tenor, Habermas is also keen to stress that his notion of moral autonomy is detailed and suggestive enough to sustain a concrete analysis and discussion. Taking our cue from Habermas's remarks in the passage quoted above, we can say that moral autonomy is exercised by the subject who shows: a) reflexivity, b) responsibility, and c) resolve. a) In order to gather and, as Habermas says, detach the self 'from the dependencies of an overwhelming environment', the subject needs to be reflexive and sensitive to the fact that this environment may prejudicially stultify or preclude the development of their autonomy. b) The subject exercises responsibility when it is prepared to give an account of its actions to the significant others with whom it has entered into 'binding commitments'. c) And, the subject acts with genuine resolve when it is unswervingly concerned to critique the reproachable aspects of a past life, and when it looks to the future with a determination to recognize itself, as Habermas would say, 'without shame'. Of course, Habermas would be the first to acknowledge that the exercise of such moral autonomy — of this kind of reflexivity, responsibility and resolve — is never an easy matter. Indeed, it is important that we bear in mind that moral autonomy is never a gift unproblematically bequeathed to the subject, but it is always the product of an active struggle. Further still from a Habermasian perspective, we should note that this active struggle for moral autonomy is made more difficult by the presence and influence of forms of ideology that function to repress or suppress it. Let us, bearing in mind these caveats, take each of the three aspects of moral autonomy in turn.

First, then, let us think about the concept of *reflexivity*. Or, more particularly, let us think about how the reflexivity of the subject may be suppressed under the undue influence of ideology. Now, the moral uneasiness with which we look on the idea of a subject whose capacity for autonomous and critical reflection is thwarted by a stultifying environment is, in a sense, quite intuitive and familiar. Indeed, we could note that the image of an unreflective and ideologically constrained subject is one that, for instance, popular Hollywood cinema constantly trades on. One example will suffice for illustrative purposes here: Gary Ross's *Pleasantville* (1998). The community of Pleasantville, as a macro or communal subject, is shown to be ideologically stultified to the extent that it is repressed by parochialism and an almost puritanical desire to maintain the status quo. This repression causes tension and conflict in the community precisely because it precludes the kind of free self-exploration and critical reflection that is so vital to the development of any autonomous sense of self. One of the key points of the film – perhaps its central intuition or contention – is that the thirst for autonomy in self-exploration and critical reflection is unquenchable or is irrepressibly anchored in the structure of subjectivity; and that this will inevitably lead to the disruption of the ideological status quo.[29]

Turning explicitly to the text of *Pleasantville* we can see how the tensions between ideological parochialism/conservatism and the desire for self-exploratory or reflexive autonomy are concretely played out. The ideological parochialism or conservatism that lingers and grips Pleasantville is perhaps most clearly expressed through the character 'Big Bob'. As a (self-appointed) community and business leader, Big Bob takes upon himself the responsibility of maintaining the standards and values of the community against what he sees as the rising tide of moral degeneration and anomie. Of course, such a supposedly moral stance is ideologically complicated by the fact that it is predicated on the idea that the status quo is self-evidently 'good'; that it must be sustained in its traditional form at all costs. This conservative argument in favour of the goodness of inherited communal values receives an explicit articulation in a scene at Pleasantville's bowling alley where Big Bob finally convinces a number of fellow citizens of the need to take decisive action against those who would challenge the traditional values that have, as he says, hitherto 'made Pleasantville great'. Disgusted by the moral degradation that surrounds him – he is dismayed by the fact that his (exclusively male) friends can no longer rely on their spouses to effectively perform the simple domestic duties required of them – Big Bob garners a fraternal support that is simply and clearly unaware of its patriarchal assumptions. Of course, this scene provokes such a critical response by playing with the hermeneutical distance that separates us as a late twentieth-century or early twenty-first-century audience from the male protagonists who –

labouring under a 1950s American 'sitcom' ideology of traditional 'family values' – are blissfully ignorant of their own sexism.[30]

The task of observing from a critical distance the curious and provocative ideological assumptions of mid-twentieth-century small-town America is something that is thrust upon the central figure of the film. David, a late twentieth-century teenager, is literally sucked through his television and transported to Pleasantville. Joining him in this world of a 1950s American sitcom is his sister Jennifer. David, or Bud as he becomes in the film or show, is simultaneously seduced and disturbed by Pleasantville – being comforted by the security of the small-town American idyll which, in another sense, suffocates him. And this tension or movement – of being both complicit and critical of the values or ideological assumptions of Pleasantville – is not peculiar to Bud's experience, but is something that resonates across a number of the other principal characters in the film. Take, for example, Bud's mum Betty. Betty initially appears as the quintessential mid-twentieth-century American housewife. She cheerfully bakes, cooks, cleans and attends to the whims of her husband and children. However, she grows disenchanted with her situation, and becomes reflexively concerned to explore a sense of self that is free from the confines of her role as a domestic housewife. This desire for freedom is expressed most dramatically by her decision to leave the marital home. Refusing point-blank to adopt the role attributed to her by George, her husband, Betty is no longer totally seduced by the ideological image of herself as a dutiful wife. Yet, for all this, her continuing complicity with the patriarchal value system of Pleasantville is reflected by the fact that she cannot bring herself to leave George without first preparing a number of 'ready-meals', or 'TV dinners', for him.

Let us come back to Habermas. Three points are worth making or emphasizing. First, Habermas would undoubtedly concur with the suggestion that the thirst for autonomy in self-exploration and critical reflection is unquenchable or is irrepressibly anchored in the structure of subjectivity. *Pleasantville*, in this Habermasian regard, projects an image of the subject that appeals to our normative intuitions.[31] Further, and second, *Pleasantville* also sensitizes us to the fact that ideology can constrain subjects by operating through discourses that make a supposedly 'objective' appeal to tradition, or to the inherited values of the community. From a Habermasian perspective, the critical difficulty or problem with making such an appeal to tradition is that it is essentially unreflective. It is never enough to assume the 'authority' of tradition precisely because tradition itself may, as Habermas says, function as a 'medium of domination and social power', serving to ideologically 'legitimate relations of organised force'.[32] This, of course, is why Big Bob's appeal to traditional values is ideologically problematic – he simply takes for granted the inherent goodness or authority of tradition, never reflecting on the fact that his cherished traditional values are pervaded by patriarchal assumptions and values. Therefore, and this is the third point, the birth of moral autonomy, and the corresponding ideology critique of tradition, are only possible through the kind of critical reflection that allows the subject to distance itself from hitherto traditionally accepted notions of the 'good'. That critically reflexive characters such as Bud and Betty are at least partly seduced by traditional forms of the 'good' or 'authority' – in Bud's case the appeal and security of the small-town American idyll, or in Betty's case the pull of her role as a domestic housewife – shows that this process is fraught with difficulty. Indeed, it is important to acknowledge, with Habermas, that the ideological 'prejudices' of tradition continue to remain a powerful stumbling block when it comes to the development of moral autonomy in the subject.[33]

Tradition, understood in this sense as the sedimentation and uncritical acceptance of ideological prejudice, is equally problematic when we come to think about the notion of *responsibility*. This is because the exercise of responsibility or, what Habermas also calls, 'responsible action' would be impossible without a measure of reflexivity on the part of the subject. Again, Habermas's argument here intuitively appeals to his ideas concerning the communicative nature of subjectivity and reason. That is to say, responsibility acquires its meaning and shape in dialogue or through communicative exchange. Or, better still, we engage in 'responsible action' to the extent that we are prepared to give an account of our actions in a discourse that is rationally motivated and reflexively open to contestation and critique.[34] Of course, failure to act in this responsible and reflexive manner inevitably risks the subjective slide into ideology. In other words, failure to rationally justify or account for one's actions to significant others – that is, others with whom we have entered into 'binding commitments' – is irresponsibly ideological. A good example of this, again from *Pleasantville*, comes in the scene where George tries to lay down the law to Betty concerning what he sees as her domestic role in the household. Earnestly engaged in the office of instructing his wife what she ought to do – 'You will have dinner, on this table at six o'clock every night . . .' – George is simply unconscious of the ridiculousness of his demands, their clear lack of any reasonable or rational foundation. From a Habermasian point of view, we could say that George's discourse is 'systematically distorted' by a form of ideology that unthinkingly or mechanically guides his actions and shapes his intentions, and which, consequently, seeks to domesticate and suppress the autonomy of Betty.[35]

Of course, Betty refuses to adopt the role that George attributes to her. In the Habermasian terms used above, we could argue that she shows a genuine *resolve* to act only in accordance with her sense of what constitutes a worthy life: that is to say, to act in those ways which allow her to recognize herself 'without shame'. Central to this process – that is, the birth of moral autonomy in Betty – is her becoming progressively and unashamedly aware of her own sexuality. Consider, for example, the scene in which we find Betty and her daughter, Jennifer (or Mary-Sue as she becomes in the film or show), engaged in a rather odd discourse about sex. The oddness or provocation of this scene is reflected in the fact that it is Mary-Sue or Jennifer who is the senior partner in the exchange. That is to say, Mary-Sue/Jennifer offers maternal advice to the inexperienced and sexually curious Betty. This exchange makes sense in the context of the narrative because Mary-Sue/Jennifer's perspective is that of a late twentieth-century teenager, and the advice and knowledge imparted by her is implicitly understood by the viewer against the post-feminist value-system or set of assumptions with which she views the world. In this way, the dialogue between Mary-Sue/Jennifer and Betty is cross-generational as much as it is intimately personal, as the hermeneutical distance and ideological tension that exists between Mary-Sue/Jennifer's post-feminism and Betty's pre-feminist experiences and understandings is sharply brought into focus. And it is this ideological tension – that is, between a pre-feminist domestication and post-feminist sexual curiosity – that importantly animates the movements of Betty as a character. For instance, her movement away from George, and her increasing curiosity regarding Mr Johnson, is clearly sexual in orientation and motivation, as the latter is unselfconsciously intrigued by her as a sexual being. Or, to make the point in a slightly different way, Betty is drawn to Mr Johnson because his actions reflect an idea that is very close to her heart: namely, that there is no shame in being regarded as an object of desire or beauty.[36]

Let us now bring our discussion of the Habermasian notion of moral autonomy, and indeed this third chapter, to a close. The central point to emerge from the above discussion is that Habermas's 'critical conception of ideology' or ideology critique is inflected with a clear moral sense; that ideology is criticizable precisely because it operates as a constraint upon the moral autonomy of subjects. This, of course, is another way of saying that the development and exercise of moral autonomy is crucial to maintain if we harbour any ambition to critique the forms of ideology that pervade social life. Yet again, it is imperative that we understand this intuition against the backcloth of Habermas's communication theory. By insisting that moral autonomy can only be exercised in and through communicative action, and that individual freedom and social reciprocity is built into the fabric of linguistically mediated interaction, Habermas is arguing that we have the dialogical or discursive resources to structure our social relations in a way that essentially frees us from the grip of ideology. That different forms of 'technocratic consciousness' or the 'prejudices' of 'tradition' continue to exert an ideological influence on social life is, in Habermas's view, a clear failing of our moral or normative intuitions. It is a failure on the part of 'we' speech actors to do justice to the moral content or structure of the communicative relations through which we inevitably invest meaning in the social world.

4 • Žižek's Ideology Theory

Slavoj Žižek's ideology theory is, in a manner similar to Habermas's, intuitively guided by the idea that a critical distinction can be drawn between the ideological and the real. Žižek, in other words, maps out one of the key features of what is, in our terms, a 'critical conception of ideology'. Of course, the way in which he theorizes this is markedly different and inevitably idiosyncratic. Rather than drawing on language philosophy to argue for a communicative conception of the real, Žižek, contra Habermas, draws heavily on the thought of Jacques Lacan to argue for, what we can call, a psychoanalytically inflected conception of 'the Real'.[1] It is crucial that we become aware of how precisely Žižek distinguishes this concept of 'the Real' from, what he also calls after a Lacanian fashion, 'the symbolic', as this provides an important key to his understanding of how 'the Real' can be distinguished from the ideological. Two points are worth broadly emphasizing in order to anticipate Žižek's thinking in this respect. First, ideology circulates within the realm of 'the symbolic' – essentially operating by structuring the meaning we invest in 'social reality'. As will become clear toward the end of the chapter, one of the most crucial ways in which ideology can symbolically structure or project a certain image of social reality is through the use of what Žižek calls 'fantasy'. Second, if ideology, for Žižek, can assume meaning and significance in 'the symbolic' by structuring or projecting a certain image of social reality, then it is in 'the Real' that this fixity of meaning will break down. That is to say, Žižek wants to argue for a notion of 'the Real' that essentially disrupts the smooth and symbolic operation of ideology. As we shall see, he refers to this experience of 'the Real' as the 'antagonism' at the heart of all ideological discourses. In this crucial sense, 'the Real' marks the limit of the ideological; bearing witness, Žižek would contend, to the fragility or contestability of the meanings and assumptions that sustain ideological images of social reality.

Before we can even begin to make sense of these claims on Žižek's behalf, it is important that I prepare the ground for a proper and concrete understanding of his concepts of 'the Real' and 'the symbolic';

that I provide some background that anticipates his thinking on these matters. This is what I try to do in the first and second parts of the chapter. In the first part of the chapter, I will focus on a Žižekian account of reason, before exploring, in the second part, his theory of subjectivity. A number of psychoanalytically inflected concepts that are crucial to understanding Žižek's ideology theory will emerge from these explorations – concepts such as 'fantasy', 'antagonism', 'subjectivization' and 'subjective destitution'. The question of how these concepts relate to 'the Real' and 'the symbolic', and how they can be mapped more broadly in conjunction with his theory of ideology, will be the focus of my concern in the third and final part of the chapter. Further, my consideration of the concept of 'the Real' in the concluding part of this fourth chapter will also help underscore just how crucial the notion is to Žižek's particular form of critical theory. For it is no exaggeration to say that the importance of 'the Real' to Žižek is virtually impossible to overestimate; that it resonates through all his writing and thinking. Indeed, we shall see as much in chapter 5 when we come to think about the kind of ethics that are implied by Žižek's critique of ideology.

Reason and fantasy

In an important recent book, *The Plague of Fantasies*, Žižek provides us with an interesting, if at times rather oblique, conception of reason.[2] Or, to put it more specifically, Žižek understands and analyses the status, scope and function of reason in a somewhat indirect, even awry, fashion by theorizing it against the background of an exploration of the notion of fantasy. Essentially, Žižek wants to argue that fantasy can condition reason, or can shape and crucially affect how reason is used in the social world. The function of fantasy is, as Žižek puts it, to 'plague' or 'blur one's clear reasoning'.[3] Fantasy, in this regard, is something that gets in the way of our using reason to look at, or see, the social world in an unproblematic fashion: it operates as a 'blind spot' in our field of vision, as Žižek might say. So we can see that the notion of reason is, for Žižek, a problematic one, or that rationality as a concept is treated problematically precisely because it is viewed as something that is supported by fantasy. Now, in order to make sense of Žižek's problematization of reason, this claim that our reasoning about the world is plagued or blurred by fantasy, we first need to develop a sense of how fantasy works or operates in social life. Žižek elaborates, what he calls, the 'contours' of the 'notion of fantasy' in resolutely 'psychoanalytical' terms. Let us, then, begin by specifying, with Žižek, some of the features that he attributes to this psychoanalytical concept of fantasy.

The first thing that we should take cognizance of, Žižek argues, is that fantasy is not simply a mere form of hallucination, a kind of daydreaming removed from reality; but is, rather, very much a part of the fabric of reality that it helps to condition. The reason for this is because fantasy shapes or, as Žižek puts it, 'constitutes our desire'.[4] In order to render this notion more concrete, we can, as Žižek does, draw on a case reported by Freud of his daughter fantasizing about eating a strawberry cake. Now, for Žižek, it would be tempting, but ultimately mistaken, to understand this as a simple case of daydreaming or hallucinatory satisfaction: that is, that the girl wanted a cake; that she could not have it in reality; so then she fantasized about eating it. Against the notion that the cake is the unreal or hallucinatory object of the girl's desire, Žižek argues that she is making herself a real object of desire by pretending to eat the cake. How so? This is because she recognizes that her parents draw great delight from viewing her ravenously eating a strawberry cake, and thereby she is making herself a real object of their desire to the extent that she precipitates in them an experience of parental enjoyment. Ultimately, then, the fantasy that constitutes the girl's desire for the strawberry cake is, at least for Žižek, anchored in a desire to be the object of parental affection.[5]

What this example shows is, what Žižek terms, 'the radically intersubjective character of fantasy'. In other words, the proper meaning of the girl's fantasy can only be apprehended when we realize that the desire structured by fantasy never totally or truly belongs to the self, but is, properly speaking, the desire of the other (in this case, the parents who desire to see their child satisfied and fulfilled). 'The original question of desire', says Žižek in this regard, 'is not "What do I want?", but "What do others want from me? What do they see in me? What am I to others?"'[6] The broader social and political implications of these questions of desire are sharply, and somewhat disturbingly, brought into focus by Žižek when he uses them as a backcloth against which to discuss 'anti-Semitism' or, what he also calls, 'anti-Semitic paranoia'. Understood in the formal sense articulated by Žižek, anti-Semitism or anti-Semitic paranoia is predicated on the notion of a 'Jewish plot' that is taken to threaten the fabric of society; or, as that which precipitates the corrosion and corruption of the core values of the organic social bond. Put simply, then, the logic of anti-Semitism as a political discourse operates in accordance with the following injunction: 'the Jew' is a disease debilitating the social body, and must be removed from it! Now, what precisely does this anti-Semitic discourse have to do with the 'radically intersubjective character of fantasy'? Well, according to Žižek, the notion of a 'Jewish plot' is an 'exemplary' case of an intersubjective or 'social fantasy' that allows the anti-Semite to answer the question concerning the desire of the other. Now, the 'other', in this case, is, Žižek points out, 'society' itself, and what it desires in this context is the maintenance of its organic well-being, purged, as it must be, of the 'Jew' that ceaselessly and pathologically threatens it.[7]

Clearly, Žižek's suggestion that anti-Semitic paranoia is structured by a social fantasy is meant immediately to signal the fact that fantasy is far from benign or merely salutary in its socio-political effects or function. This brings us neatly to another feature that he attributes to fantasy: namely, that it operates in a social field to suppress or occlude, what he calls, 'antagonism'.[8] Anti-Semitic paranoia or, what Žižek more generally calls, 'fascism' is a political discourse seduced by the fantasy of a form of political power or authority that thinks itself impervious to antagonism. We see this clearly, argues Žižek, in the kind of 'corporatist vision' of society that it articulates. Put simply, the corporatist vision articulated by fascism strongly implies an image of political society as an 'organic Whole', or as 'a social Body in which the different classes are like extremities, members each contributing to the whole'.[9] Now, this image of society is a fantasy-image to the extent that it implies a form of political power, authority and, ultimately, order that is not split by antagonistic struggle, social upheaval, competition, or any kind of political unrest. As Žižek clearly points out, this projected image of a fascist political society in which everyone is pulling together, where there is no antagonism between social actors, where every member of society contributes collectively to the greater good, is obviously rendered problematic by the presence of the 'Jew' who is considered, as he says, 'the foreign body introducing corruption into the social fabric'. Žižek's psychoanalytical point here is that this fantasy-creation or figure of the 'Jew' acts as a kind of shock-absorber or scapegoat on to which the ills of society are projected. In a way, there is a kind of 'displacement' at work whereby 'social antagonism' – the fact that there are power struggles, competition among actors for scarce resources, deep class, racial, gender divisions and so on – 'condenses' around the figure of the 'Jew' who alone is offered as the source of social strife and unrest. The clear consequence of this, for Žižek, is that the genuine sources or causes of antagonism in social life are phantasmically removed from view; hidden as they are behind the smoke-screen of anti-Semitic paranoia.[10]

Fantasy does not only allow us as social actors to repress and remove things from view; it also allows us to view things that are not, strictly speaking, possible to see. Fantasy can involve the adoption of, what Žižek terms, an 'impossible gaze': for example, 'the gaze by means of which the subject is present at the act of his/her own conception'.[11] This kind of fantasy-scenario is something that we find exemplified in narrative literature: the novel and novella being obvious examples.[12] Žižek himself animates this notion of an 'impossible gaze' by drawing on, what he calls, 'an anti-abortion fairytale written . . . by a right-wing Slovene nationalist poet'. The tale is staged, Žižek tells us, on an idyllic South Sea island where aborted children live together, and where they melancholically reflect on the fact that their parents did not want or seem to need them. By reading this narrative as a 'right-wing' and 'anti-abortion fairytale', Žižek is undoubtedly concerned to analyse it as a piece of political propaganda. Indeed, the whole point of the narrative, as far as Žižek is concerned, is that it constructs a fantasy-scenario whereby the 'impossible gaze' of the aborted children can be reflected back as a 'reproachful gaze' to the parents who betrayed them, consequently making them feel guilty for having acted so selfishly. Therefore, it is crucial, from a Žižekian perspective, to bear in mind that the political significance of this fantasy-narrative is reflected in the fact that it is motivated by the prospect of shaping or conditioning the minds of social actors in a clear way: that is, of convincing them that abortion is immoral and selfish.[13]

So we see that the features that Žižek attributes to the notion of fantasy, coupled with the provocative, disturbing and morally problematic examples he uses to animate his discussion, leave the clear impression that it is, as we said above, far from a benign phenomenon. Indeed, perhaps the lasting impression that Žižek leaves us with is that fantasy is a political phenomenon, and that a proper understanding of fantasy always-already presupposes a form of analysis that tries to tease out its political significance and consequences. But what, we need to ask, does this notion of fantasy have to do with the idea of reason? Or, rephrasing the question again, what can the political phenomenon of fantasy tells us about the concept of reason? In light of what we have already seen, the argument to be drawn out is this: if fantasy is, as Žižek clearly implies, potentially politically dangerous and morally problematic, and if fantasy 'plagues' our use of reason in the social world, then the exercise of reason is itself potentially politically dangerous and morally problematic. In a sense, of course, this is already implicit in Žižek's critical analysis. That is to say, we have already seen how the 'paranoid anti-Semite' essentially *reasons* that the removal of the 'Jew' is the best way to maintain the organic social bond. Or how, to take another example, the 'right-wing anti-abortionist' essentially *reasons* that abortion is immoral and selfish. Ultimately, the implication of Žižek's argument is simple: to use reason is to engage in a potentially perilous and hazardous act – tread carefully![14]

But is this the whole story? Is Žižek, contra Habermas for example, ultimately pessimistic about the status, scope and function of reason? Or does he hold out for the possibility that we can reason in a way that moves beyond or, as he would say, 'traverses' the 'plague' of fantasy? It is important to acknowledge the fact that Žižek always-already presupposes such a move beyond fantasy is possible by engaging in a political critique of it. For instance, against the 'anti-Semitic' fantasy that the 'Jew' is the source of 'social antagonism', Žižek would suggest that the source of antagonism in social life can be more realistically found in the economic distribution of wealth and resources: 'It's the Political Economy, Stupid' is his amusing play on Clinton's election sound-bite.[15] Or, against the 'right-wing anti-abortionist' fantasy or idea that abortion is typically or disproportionately the act of an immoral and selfish career woman, Žižek would suggest that abortion is more often the last realistic option facing poor women who already have a number of children to support.[16] So it is clear that, in both cases, Žižek attempts to critically locate a blind spot in the field of the fantasist's vision – 'anti-Semite' and 'anti-abortionist' – while simultaneously reasoning that more clarity can be brought to bear on the issue at hand.

Let me now sum up the main points that follow from this discussion of the Žižekian notions of fantasy and reason. The first, and perhaps most obvious, point is that reason is a problematic concept to the extent that it is anchored in, what we could call, the politically dangerous and morally problematic world of fantasy. Yet, fantasy can be exposed as politically dangerous or morally problematic, and the forms of reason or rationality supported by fantasy – 'anti-Semitic' for example – can be questioned, even denounced, by the critic who is sensitive to their blind spots. Therefore, there is a possibility that we can reason, that reason can be used, in a way that allows us to critique the rationality of the fantasist. Indeed, what Žižek offers us here is a reasoned critique of reason, or, put another way, a negative critique of one form of fantasy-plagued reasoning which must assume a more rational way of looking at things. But what kind of rationality does Žižek have in mind here? What characterizes the form of reasoning that allows us to move beyond or 'traverse' fantasy? These are questions that I will come back to in the third, and final, part of the chapter. But before so doing, it will prove useful to shift the focus of our attention somewhat by giving due consideration to Žižek's theory of subjectivity. This is not to imply that Žižek's concept of the subject bears no connection or relevance to what has been said here in relation to the notion of fantasy. Indeed, we shall see, again in the concluding part of the chapter, how the Žižekian concepts of fantasy and subjectivity tie into one another.

Subjectivization and subjective destitution

Žižek reserves something of a special and privileged place for his conception of the subject. The product of long and powerfully theoretical meditations, and marked by an unashamedly philosophical depth and intensity, Žižek's notion of subjectivity hardly presents itself in an easily accessible form.[17] That said, Žižek's theory of subjectivity undoubtedly has a clear focus in the sense that he is motivated by the desire to understand, what we could call, the politics of subjectivity. By this I mean that Žižek is concerned to analyse the process through which subjects are caught in the grip of a certain kind of political constraint or subjugation – he refers to this as 'subjectivization'. In the course of meditating on this idea of subjectivization, Žižek, we shall see, engages with the work of Louis Althusser and with, what he terms, the 'post-Althusserian political philosophy' of figures such as Alain Badiou and Jacques Rancière. Ultimately critical of Althusser and post-Althusserian political philosophy, Žižek insists that there is something in the structure of subjectivity that can enable the subject to break free from the deadlock of political constraint or subjugation. Drawing creatively on the psychoanalytical theory of Lacan, Žižek contends that such freedom is indeed within the grasp of the subject who is prepared to, as he would put it, 'embrace the act' of 'subjective destitution'. Let us, then, first focus on the issue of subjectivization, before turning, towards the end of this second part of the chapter, to the provocative notion of subjective destitution. In one of his most impressive books to date, *The Ticklish Subject*, Žižek provides an in-depth exploration of the concept of 'subjectivization'.[18] The first thing that we should immediately note concerning Žižek's analysis of subjectivization is that he is, much as in his analysis of fantasy, concerned to understand it as a political phenomenon. This, as I have already intimated, is a lesson that Žižek takes implicitly and explicitly from Louis Althusser. That is to say, in Althusser Žižek finds a developed theory of 'political subjectivization' or, what he also calls, 'political subjectivity' that continues to exercise a decisive influence over contemporary social and political theory. So what, therefore, are the important features of Althusser's theory of political subjectivity? And, further, what precisely is the nature of the influence that Althusser continues to exert over contemporary thinking on this matter? Let us take the first question first. Althusser's theory of political subjectivity is inextricably linked to his well-known theory of 'interpellation' as 'hailing'. The, now famous and often-quoted, example that Althusser gives to animate this idea is that of a policeman who hails an individual by shouting: 'Hey, you there!' Now, by recognizing this hailing, by turning round and turning oneself into an addressee, the individual, from an Althusserian perspective, 'becomes a subject', the bearer of a form of political subjectivity. Althusser describes this process of 'interpellation' thus:

> Assuming that the theoretical scene I have imagined [that of the policeman shouting 'Hey, you there!'] takes place in the street, the hailed individual will turn round. By this mere one-hundred-and-eighty-degree physical conversion, he becomes a *subject*. Why? Because he has recognized that the hail was 'really' addressed to him, and that 'it was really him who was hailed' (and not someone else). Experience shows that the practical telecommunication of hailings is such that they hardly ever miss their man . . . the one hailed always recognizes that it is really him who is being hailed.[19]

It is interesting to note how Althusser refers to the hailed individual or 'subject' as the one who recognizes that the hail is 'really' being addressed to her/him. Why, though, does he put the word 'really' in scare quotes here? This is clearly an ironic allusion, which is, in fact, meant to signify that the 'interpellated' subject is labouring under a serious misconception: that the subject's recognition of the hail is, paradoxically, predicated on, what Althusser would call, a fundamental 'misrecognition' of the fact that the hail itself has none of the supposedly necessary authority that is granted to it by the individual in the first instance. This brings us neatly to another important feature of Althusser's theory of subject: namely, that political subjectivity has an important 'imaginary' aspect to the extent that it is constituted in accordance with a form of authority that we envision is justified without question. Although it is necessary to acknowledge that this 'imaginariness', as Althusser would say, is not simply the product of an individual's conscious imaginings as such; but is, more fundamentally, a matter of social, political and, ultimately, institutional 'material' practice. Therefore, the reason that the 'interpellated' individual subjects itself to the hailing of the policeman, the reason that our individual consciously or unconsciously defers to the policeman's authority, is that the latter speaks from a position of legal-institutional authority. The policeman's power to interpellate individuals, in other words, is reflected in the fact that s/he is part of, what Althusser calls, the 'apparatus' of the 'state'.[20]

So, returning to the second question posed above, what precisely is the nature of the influence that Althusser continues to exert over contemporary theorizations of political subjectivity? Looking specifically at the work of contemporary political philosophers such as Alain Badiou and Jacques Rancière, Žižek detects a residual, but nonetheless significant, Althusserianism on each of their parts. Although, at first sight at least, the political philosophies of Badiou and Rancière would seem to be defined by a kind of negative and critical relationship to Althusser: that is, by the way their theories of political subjectivity express, as Žižek says, 'different ways of negating' or 'gaining a distance' from an explicitly Althusserian approach.[21] One way of emphasizing this difference or distinction would be to stress, with Žižek, how Althusser was, in the last analysis, pessimistic and dismissive about the prospect of developing a form of subjectivity that could escape the subjugating influence of the 'state apparatus': that, in an important sense, being a subject, or having subjectivity, necessarily or always involves the 'misrecognition' of state authority as 'really' justified, rather than seeing it as simply 'imaginary'. Against this Althusserian pessimism, Badiou and Rancière are engaged in the theorization of forms of political subjectivity that they consider fundamentally challenging to the authority of the state.[22]

Let us focus first and briefly on Badiou, or, more accurately, on Žižek's treatment of Badiou. As Žižek shows, Badiou insists on a crucial distinction, or substantive difference, between the state and the subject. And it is necessary to point out that this distinction between the state and the subject is, from Badiou's perspective, grounded on the basis of a more fundamental difference between, what he terms, 'being' and 'event'; that is to say, where the state belongs to the order of being, the subject is defined by its relation to the event. In order to make sense of this crucial Badiouian distinction between being and event, Žižek takes the example of the 'order of being' that was late eighteenth-century French society, and the way it was rocked by the 'event' of the 'French Revolution'. The French society of the late eighteenth-century had not only a 'state apparatus' – the state of the *ancien regime* that was about to implode – but a more general 'state of society', reflecting a certain kind of societal 'situation' that can be accounted for and made accessible to, what Žižek following Badiou calls, 'knowledge'. Yet, and this is the crucial thing, out of the reach of knowledge, and out of the reach and influence of 'the state', we have the wholly contingent, unpredictable and unforeseen 'event' of the 'French Revolution' which intervenes in the 'order of being' in such a way as to strike at its very heart, ultimately precipitating the structural breakdown and collapse of 'the state' or *ancien regime*. So, how, then, does the subject figure in the 'event' that is this structural breakdown of the state? Drawing explicitly on Badiou, Žižek maintains that the subject is defined, that political subjectivity is defined, by 'a *fidelity* to the event'.[23] For Žižek, the importance of this idea of the subject's 'fidelity' to the 'event' is that it bears witness to the idea that wholesale restructuring of the political sphere is possible; that the 'state' of any given society can be comprehensively disassembled; that the political authority of the state can be revealed as nothing other than a product of the imaginings of those subject to it; that, ultimately, the political 'miracle', as he calls it, of radical societal change can happen.[24]

As in the case of Badiou, Žižek discerns in Rancière a clear insistence on the kind of subjectivity that functions to challenge, and antagonize, the smooth running of the state apparatus. The crucial distinction that emerges from this Žižekian reading of Rancière concerns the difference between, what we could call, the policed subject and the politicized subject. The difference is this: where the policed subject is subjugated to, or circumscribed within, the norms, codes and conventions of the established social order, the politicized subject attempts to establish a new order as such, a change in the public sphere that accommodates a hitherto marginalized voice. To the extent that the politicized subject insists on opening up the public sphere, and on the accommodation of the dissenting voice, it is engaged in a process of democratization. Properly speaking, then, the politicized subject is, from this perspective, a democratizing subject.[25] Now Rancière's problem with the state, as Žižek reads it, is that it tends to operate in accordance with a 'police' logic which consequently functions not to politicize, but to essentially depoliticize the public sphere by insisting that there is no need for change; that, as Žižek ironically says, 'things should go back to normal'. Of course, by putting the suggestion that 'things should go back to normal' in scare quotes Žižek is keen to bring into focus the inherently conservative and 'anti-democratic' nature of this police logic. That is to say, the political subtext of 'things should go back to normal' is, in effect, 'shut up, your dissension, and calls for change, are simply getting in the way of the smooth functioning of the status-quo!'[26]

Taken together, then, the post-Althusserian political philosophy of Badiou and Rancière is motivated by the prospect of developing a form of political subjectivity that seeks autonomy from the subjugating influence of the state. By emphasizing how a subject's faith in the 'event' bears witness to the possibility of radical societal change, and by suggesting that those marginalized within a state or political community can refashion it so as to accommodate their hitherto silenced voice, both Badiou and Rancière, Žižek contends, insist that state power and authority can be subject to direct critique. On the face of it, then, Badiou and Rancière would seem to be 'radical' political thinkers, at least in the sense that they want to maintain a critical scepticism apropos state power and authority. Žižek, though, would caution us not to move too quickly or easily with such an assumption, lest we should fail to appreciate how such a supposedly 'radical' anti-statism can paradoxically imply a type of conservatism. That is to say, what Žižek detects in 'marginalist radical' thinkers such as Badiou and Rancière is essentially a lack of nerve when it comes to the crunch of articulating what should come after the critique of any given form of state authority or power: there is, he argues, a 'refusal to assume responsibility for Power'.[27] What Žižek wants to bring into focus here is the difference between merely engaging in a perpetual critique of state power and actually embracing the task of institutionalizing political change. Put simply, while figures such as Badiou and Rancière seemingly engage in a provocative and subversive undermining of state power and authority, they, in the end, risk offering nothing new or positive in the wake of such a critique.[28]

So we see that Žižek's discussion of the forms of political subjectivization or political subjectivity that he finds in Althusser and in post-Althusserian theory is, in the final analysis, essentially critical and negative in tenor. Both are, in his view, caught in the deadlock of subjugation and constraint to the degree that they fail to adequately theorize a possible critique of hegemonic power or authority.[29] It is against this backdrop that we must understand the significance of Žižek's concept of 'subjective destitution', or Žižek's contention that freedom from hegemonic power or authority is indeed within the grasp of the subject who is prepared to go through subjective destitution. What, though, does it mean for the subject to go through a process of subjective destitution? Drawing on the psychoanalytical theory of Lacan, Žižek suggests that in going through subjective destitution the subject 'no longer presupposes himself as subject', that 'he . . . annuls himself as subject'.[30] Whatever could this challengingly cryptic remark mean? What Žižek is hinting at here is the possibility that a subject can cut itself loose from the social networks of meaning in which it is inscribed and constrained; that it could free itself from all that it had hitherto invested with sense and value; that it could freely bear all the painful consequences that follow from refusing to give way to the will of those in possession of power. This kind of 'act', as Žižek calls it, is something we often find dramatized in cinema or film, where a central protagonist 'acts' with such freedom, such a wilful resolve, so as to effectively strike out at all that had been previously held dear. Consider, for example, Žižek's analysis of the flashback scene in Bryan Singer's *The Usual Suspects* (1995), when:

> the mysterious Keyser Soeze returns home and finds his wife and small daughter held at gunpoint by the members of a rival mob, and he resorts to the radical gesture of shooting his wife and daughter . . . this act enables him mercilessly to pursue members of the rival gang, their families, parents and friends, killing them all . . . This act, far from amounting to a case of impotent aggressivity turned against oneself, rather changes the coordinates of the situation in which the subject finds himself: by cutting himself loose from the precious object through whose possession the enemy kept him in check, the subject gains the space of free action.[31]

Cut loose from the social-symbolic universe in which he finds himself, and possessing the will and courage to make the choice of killing his family and thereby retaining his freedom from the blackmailing rival mob, Soeze, on Žižek's provocative reading, radically alters the circumstances that give shape to his predicament. As ever, Žižek is concerned to tease out what he considers to be the political implications or consequences of engaging in such an 'act' of subjective destitution. The issue is this: if, as Žižek suggests, the shared and seemingly imperishable meanings and values we invest in the social-symbolic network can be momentarily suspended by the subject, then this must be equally true of the meanings and values that govern our political life. Žižek, again drawing creatively on Lacan, would refer to this as the subject's insistence on 'the non-existence of the big Other'.[32] That is to say, by insisting on the 'non-existence of the big Other', the subject declares that the supposed symbolic authority of the values that are unquestionably taken to govern social life are merely exposed for what they are: namely, as fabrications, imaginings which, in truth, only carry authority to the extent that they are invested with meaning and significance by subjects in the first place.[33] Or, to bring it back to Žižek's filmic example, Soeze insists on the 'non-existence of the big Other' by directly attacking the symbolic authority assumed by the rival blackmailing gang. Of course, they must have imagined that Soeze would give way to their demands: but he doesn't, he 'embraces the act', as Žižek would say, and takes the almost unbearably painful option of freedom through subjective destitution.

Leaving aside the clear moral provocation implied by Žižek's adoption of Soeze as a kind of heroic and radically autonomous figure, we can content ourselves, at least for the time being, by reinforcing one final and rather obvious point: namely, that subjective freedom comes at a price.[34] That is to say, to embrace the act or go through the process of subjective destitution, the subject, from a Žižekian perspective, must suffer an almost unbearable pain. Freedom is horrible, horrendous even, and cutting oneself loose from the social-symbolic network is almost unthinkable. It is, as Žižek says, like making what seems an 'impossible' choice.[35] All of this amounts to saying that the act of subjective destitution brings us into contact with, what Žižek famously and elliptically calls, 'the Real'. Now, this concept of 'the Real' is, as I indicated at the beginning of the chapter, the problematic and paradoxical idea around which all Žižek's thinking crucially turns. Indeed, we shall see that the notion of 'the Real' provides the intuitive backcloth against which to understand the theories or notions of fantasy and subjectivity that we have discussed thus far. Further, and most crucially for our purposes, we also shall see that the concept of 'the Real' provides the crucial starting point for coming to grips with Žižek's theory of ideology. So it is to a discussion of this most elusive and tricky concept that we must urgently direct our attention.

The real and the ideological

If the Lacanian notion of 'the Real' is the most crucial and significant of Žižek's conceptual lexicon, then this is clearly because it serves as a constant reference, permeating all his writing and argumentation. Crucial to Žižek's thinking in this respect is the development, and maintenance, of the distinction between 'the Real' and 'the symbolic'. We can, for our purposes, think of 'the symbolic' as a shared space of social meaning, or, put another way, as the sphere in which we invest meaning and significance in the world we intersubjectively inhabit. It is when 'the symbolic' breaks down, when the norms and values that sustain the shared space of social meaning are suspended, that we, as Žižek would say, encounter the 'negativity' of 'the Real'.[36] So what we have at play here apropos Žižek's differentiation of 'the Real' from 'the symbolic' is a desire to understand how the latter is destabilized by the former. Now, this kind of movement from 'the symbolic' into 'the Real', this fundamental strain between 'the symbolic' and 'the Real', is something that resonates throughout all Žižek's work. Indeed, it is, as I implied a moment ago, readily discernible in the key concepts and theories of fantasy and subjectivity that I discussed in the previous two parts of the chapter.

Let us first focus on the notion of fantasy. As I noted earlier, one of Žižek's core intuitions is that fantasy is a political phenomenon, and that a proper understanding of fantasy presupposes a form of analysis that tries to tease out its political significance and consequences. What I can now add to this intuition is Žižek's belief that the political significance and consequences that follow from participating in fantasy are played out in the realm of 'the symbolic': that is, in a shared space of social meaning. Further, we could say that fantasy plays a 'symbolic' function in social-political life when it operates through a discourse or narrative that attempts to ensure fixity of meaning and order in the latter. Indeed, all political discourses, from a Žižekian perspective, can be read as attempts to order the social world by fixing or, as he would say, 'quilting' meaning in a certain way.[37] We can again consider, by way of example, the political discourse of Žižek's 'paranoid anti-Semite'. At bottom, the political discourse of the paranoid anti-Semite is, as we have seen, anchored in the belief that the removal of the 'Jew' is the best way to maintain the organic social bond. So we are left in no doubt as to precise subtext or meaning implied by the fantasy-projection of an organic social bond being threatened by the figure of the 'Jew': namely, get rid of the 'Jew' or our political community will perish!

If fantasy functions in 'the symbolic' through political discourses that fix social meaning and order social life, then this, for Žižek, is only because they repress or deny the potentially destabilizing impact of 'the Real'. Yet, and this is a fundamental point for Žižek, 'the Real' itself can never be totally repressed or fully domesticated within 'the symbolic' precisely because the latter always retains traces of the former within it. Philosophically speaking, then, we could say, with Žižek, that 'the Real' is *immanent* to 'the symbolic'.[38] By this Žižek means that the efficiency or effectiveness of political discourses in 'the symbolic' bear, what is for him, the unavoidable or necessary trace of 'the Real' to the extent that they are indelibly marked by the prospect of their failure to unproblematically fix social meaning and order social life. The conceptual term that Žižek uses to signify this experience of 'the Real' as causing failure is one we have already encountered: namely, 'antagonism'. There is, as Žižek says, a 'central antagonism' at the heart of all political discourses to the degree that they are 'doomed to fail' in their pursuit of imposing meaning and order on 'the social'.[39] Why, according to Žižek, do they fail in this way? This is because the meanings attached to the social world, the meanings we invest in the symbolic realm, are essentially or forever contestable; and it is not possible to ever assume what Žižek calls 'a point of supreme density of Meaning' because meaning itself is never assumed, but always is presupposed and indeed 'performed' by the agent who posits it as such.[40]

This experience of antagonism, this experience of the essential contestability or fragility of meaning, this experience of 'the Real' resonating in 'the symbolic', is something that Žižek shows to be explicitly mediated through the act of political critique. In a sense, we have already witnessed this. That is to say, we have already seen how Žižek engages in a critique of political discourses that are, in his view, sustained by assumptions and meanings that are contestable. Yet again, we can consider his critique of anti-Semitism. The discourse of the anti-Semite is explicitly criticizable, according to Žižek, because it represses 'the Real' of 'antagonism', trying to displace it on to the figure of the 'Jew' who alone is 'rationally' offered as the source of social strife and unrest. Of course, from Žižek's perspective, the supposed 'rationality' of the anti-Semite is lacking and found wanting, and is accordingly revealed for the 'social fantasy' that it is. In a sense, what Žižek offers us here is a reasoned critique of reason, or, as we put it earlier, a negative critique of one form of fantasy-plagued reasoning which must assume a more rational way of looking at things. But what kind of rationality does Žižek have in mind in this context? What form of reasoning allows us to transcend or traverse fantasy? Everything pivots around the notion of 'the Real' here: for the form of reason that allows us to traverse the 'plague of fantasies' is one which touches 'the Real' or, as Žižek otherwise puts it, the 'pre-symbolic Real'. Two points are worth bearing in mind here. First, the use of reason that touches the 'pre-symbolic Real' is achieved, or is only achievable, in a gesture of 'withdrawal'. By this Žižek means that using reason to critique fantasy-plagued reasoning involves a withdrawal from the symbolic realm or network in which it assumes meaning: it involves insisting or maintaining that fantasy-plagued reason (for example, 'anti-Semitism' or 'anti-abortionism') is destabilized by the negative fact that its meaning is always-already contestable, contingent and, in this sense, failed.[41] Second, this critical use of reason bears witness to the 'pre-symbolic Real' to the degree that it is mediated through a gesture of 'symbolic (re)constitution'. By this Žižek means that using reason to critique fantasy-plagued reasoning involves the reconstruction of the image of 'social reality' that it sustains.[42] An example of this would be Žižek's own critical suggestion, mentioned earlier, that the image of social reality implied in anti-Semitic discourse – a social reality pathologically threatened by the 'Jew' – needs to be rethought, and an appreciation of the genuine sources of conflict and antagonism in social life are best analysed in terms of the distribution of wealth and economic resources.

It is necessary to emphasize how what we have said here concerning 'fantasy' and 'reason' connects up with Žižek's theory of subjectivity. Most immediately, it is simply worth acknowledging that fantasy helps constitute or create 'the subject', and that the subject has a capacity or faculty for critical reasoning. Let us separate out each of these points, taking them in their turn. In a basic sense, fantasy creates, or captures, the subject through the constitution of its 'desire': fantasy, as Žižek often likes to say, literally teaches us 'how to desire'.[43] Now, the process whereby fantasy captures the subject through the structuring of desire is one which resonates strongly with the Žižekian notion of 'subjectivization' that I discussed earlier. Casting our minds back to the Althusserian notion of the 'interpellated' subject, we can begin to see how the latter occupies a kind of fantasy-space. That is to say, by 'misrecognizing' or granting an authority to the 'hail' which issues from the 'state apparatus', the 'subject', we could say, is captured by a desire for a fantasy-image of state power as impregnable or unassailable. In the 'post-Althusserian political philosophy' of Badiou and Rancière Žižek finds a rather strange, even paradoxical, twist in this economy of desire. On the face of it, Badiou and Rancière exhibit none of the pessimism that is often taken to characterize Althusser's reflections on the subjugating influence of the state: that is, Badiou and Rancière are, as I said, concerned to develop a conception of subjectivity that functions to challenge, and antagonize, the smooth running of the state apparatus. The twist or sting in this tale, at least as Žižek has it, is that Badiou and Rancière are themselves subjugated or constrained to the degree that they are caught in a game of 'hysterical provocation'. What this means is that although Badiou and Rancière rage against the subjugating influence of the state, they do so by paradoxically imbuing it with an almost mystical power to order political life in accordance with its own, essentially instrumental, concerns and logic. Žižek's point, of course, is that this amounts to saying that the state is indeed impregnable: that Badiou and Rancière 'hysterically' desire, or are caught up in, a fantasy-image of the state as unassailably powerful.[44]

Turning to the issue of how the subject manifests a capacity or faculty for critical reasoning, it is crucial to be aware of the way in which this is tied into the Žižekian notion of subjective destitution. Or, to put it in more categorical terms: the withdrawal from, and (re)constitution of, 'the symbolic' that characterizes the critical use of reason is inextricably linked to the 'act' of subjective destitution. Think back, for instance, to Žižek's discussion of the 'mysterious' Keyser Soeze. Soeze's 'act' of killing his family in order to maintain his freedom from a blackmailing rival mob clearly involves both a withdrawal from, and (re)constitution of, 'the symbolic' realm in which he finds himself. That is to say, by cutting himself loose from 'the symbolic' – that is, the shared space of meaning that is the familial network – he is able, on this reading, to reconstruct or change his circumstances. Yet again, we find ourselves circulating within the Žižekian register of 'the Real'. That is to say, Soeze touches the 'pre-symbolic Real' through his withdrawal from, and (re)constitution of, 'the symbolic'; he bears witness to the breakdown or suspension of the 'symbolic' meaning and significance implied by deeply cherished familial relations and ties; he steadfastly refuses to be a prisoner of subjugation and constraint; he reasons with all the 'madness', as Žižek would say, of a man intent on not giving way to those who have symbolically assumed power over him.[45]

So, can we wade through Žižek's psychoanalytical musings here concerning the concepts of 'subjective destitution', 'reason', 'fantasy', 'subjectivization', 'the Real' and 'the symbolic' in order to arrive at a discernible theory of ideology? Or, putting the question more positively, how can we introduce Žižek's theory of ideology against the backcloth of the core ideas that have shaped our discussion of his thinking thus far? The first thing we could say is that fantasy, for Žižek, is irreducibly ideological, and that his incessant desire to read fantasy as a political phenomenon is at once a desire to read it ideologically. As Žižek puts it in *The Sublime Object of Ideology*: 'The fundamental level of ideology . . . is that of . . . fantasy structuring our social reality.'[46] In this way, the 'social fantasy' of the 'paranoid anti-Semite' is, Žižek would argue, thoroughly ideological precisely because it tries to structure or project a certain image of 'social reality' – again, the social reality which is supposedly threatened by the 'Jew'. And, when an ideological fantasy such as this teaches or moves us to desire this kind of 'social reality', then it really does exercise a decisive grip or 'hold' on us as subjects.[47] This brings into focus the ideological significance of the concept of 'subjectivization'. Put simply, the process of subjectivization is expressly ideological to the degree that it circumscribes the subject within a subjugating or constraining fantasy-space. This means that Althusser's 'interpellated' subject and the 'hysterical' forms of subjectivity he finds in Badiou and Rancière are understood immediately on ideological terms by Žižek: that is to say, they are all strangely seduced by an ideological image of the state as unassailably powerful. Taking together these points about the ideological significance of fantasy and subjectivization, it is important to emphasize how they both circulate within the realm of 'the symbolic'. This is another way of saying that ideology assumes its settled meaning, that ideology captures subjects within a shared fantasy-space, by essentially performing the 'symbolic' function of staging or structuring a particular sense of what constitutes the 'reality' of the social.[48]

If ideology, for Žižek, can assume settled meaning and significance in 'the symbolic', then it is in 'the Real' that this fixity of meaning will inevitably break down. So we see that 'the Real' relates to the ideological, for Žižek, much in the same way that it relates to 'the symbolic'. That is to say, there is a sense in which 'the Real' is *immanent* to the ideological. Or, put yet another way, 'the Real', as the inevitable experience of 'antagonism', is that which unavoidably or necessarily bears witness to the contingent and contestable meanings and assumptions that are at play in all ideological formations. In this way, Žižek's suggestion and practice of using reason to critique and contest the assumptions of fantasy-plagued political discourses such as 'anti-Semitism' needs immediately to be read as a critique of ideology. So against the ideology that tries to symbolically project a more or less fixed image of 'social reality', 'the Real', for Žižek, provides a space in which it is possible to mount an antagonistic challenge, to effectively say 'No!' to the lure of the fantasy-projections upon which ideology so ceaselessly trades and functions.[49] Added to this, Žižek insists on maintaining the intuition that this critical space provided by 'the Real' can be distinguished and clearly demarcated from 'the symbolic' field in which ideology operates. Put simply, 'the Real' is a space, or as Žižek prefers, 'place' in which we can wrestle free from the grip of ideology: 'the Real' signifies the possibility of gaining a critical 'distance' from the ideological.[50]

Let us sum up this fourth chapter by reinforcing a few important points, and by raising a note of caution against the Žižekian theory of ideology we have begun to introduce here. The first point is that a critical conception or understanding of the operation of ideology in social life must, from a Žižekian perspective, proceed from an analysis of its 'symbolic' function: that is to say, the critic of ideology must be sensitive to the ways in which ideology attempts to impose fixity of meaning on 'social reality'. Second, by bringing into focus the contingent and contestable meanings and assumptions that are at play in fantasized and ideological images of 'social reality', the critic of ideology touches 'the Real', or bears witness to, what Žižek would call, 'the Real' of 'antagonism'. Further, and third, the space afforded to the critic by the existence of 'the Real' is at once a space, or 'place', that marks a distance from, and a movement beyond, the grip or subjugating influence of ideology. Indeed, it is best to think of the 'place' of 'the Real' as that which is unconstrained by the ideological: 'the Real', in this sense, is a non-ideological or, better still, pre-ideological site, signifying the essential contestability and fragility of the meanings and assumptions that sustain ideological images of 'social reality'. Needless to say, this critical differentiation of 'the Real' from the ideological is predicated on the assumption that the concept of 'the Real' has the autonomy and significance that Žižek attributes to it. This, we should be clear, is an assumption that is open to question. Indeed, we shall see in the concluding chapter how Žižek's concept of 'the Real', and the distinction that he tries to draw between 'the Real' and the ideological, can be directly subjected to critical interrogation. But before we can begin to consider such a critique of 'the Real', we need to further underscore the significant role it plays in Žižek's critical theory. And this is what I intend to do in the next chapter through an exploration of the ethics that are implied by the Žižekian critique of ideology.

5 • Žižek's Ethical Critique of Ideology

In the last chapter I set about introducing Žižek's psychoanalytically inflected theory of ideology. That is to say, we saw how Žižek's analysis of ideology needs to be intuitively understood against the backcloth of Lacanian psychoanalysis. Crucial here, of course, were the twin registers of 'the symbolic' and 'the Real'. At bottom, ideology, from a Žižekian perspective, operates or assumes its social meaning and purpose by functioning within the realm of 'the symbolic'. Or, to slightly modify the point, ideology assumes its settled meaning by essentially performing the 'symbolic' function of staging or structuring a particular sense of what constitutes the 'reality' of the social. Therein lies, for Žižek, the ideological significance of fantasy: for it is through the projection of fantasy that ideology really takes shape, determining, as it does, the libidinal economy of subjects who are captured or, to use the Althusserian language employed in the last chapter, 'interpellated' by it. Yet ideology, Žižek would argue, can never absolutely or unconditionally subjugate or constrain the subject. Or, as we saw, ideology encounters an unsurpassable limit, faces the inevitability of its own breakdown, when it comes in contact with 'the Real' of 'antagonism'. One crucial point, again worth re-emphasizing, is this: 'the Real' can be thought of as a critical space or 'place' that marks a distance from, and a movement beyond, the subjugating grip of ideology or, more accurately, from 'the symbolic' field in which ideology operates. In this way, then, 'the Real' signifies the possibility of a certain kind of liberty or freedom, where 'freedom' itself is immediately understood to entail the prospect of gaining critical distance from the ideological.[1]

By referring to 'the Real' as a space of liberty or freedom I immediately bring into focus what is, for Žižek, a core feature of this most important concept: namely, that 'the Real' is inextricably tied to the ethical. Indeed, Žižek offers us the promise of, what he would call, an 'ethics of the Real'.[2] Or, put more strongly, the practice of 'ethics' is, in Žižek's view, impossible to adequately conceptualize without reference to 'the Real'. 'Ethics', as he puts it, designates or implies a certain 'fidelity' to 'the Real'.[3] Understood from the point of view of Žižek's theory and critique of ideology, the significance of this intuition should be clear enough. For if 'the Real' provides a space in which it is possible to mount a critique of ideology, and if 'the Real' is inextricably tied to the ethical, then we must expect Žižek's ideology critique or 'critical conception of ideology' to have a significant and defining ethical aspect. Put simply, we should expect to see that Žižek is motivated by the prospect of formulating an ethical critique of ideology. And this is precisely what we will see as this fifth chapter develops. In order to suggest that an ethical critique of ideology is possible, Žižek must automatically assume that a qualitative distinction can be made between what is, properly speaking, *ethical*, and what is merely *ideological*. Two examples of how Žižek articulates or expresses this intuition are worth dwelling on, and will prove instructive here. First, we can look to the critical distinction that Žižek draws between, what we can call, 'ethical responsibility' and the 'ideology of totalitarianism'. This will be the focus of our attention in the first part of the chapter. From here, I will move, in the second part of the chapter, to a discussion of the critical distinction that Žižek would draw between, what we can call, 'ethical belief' and the 'ideology of cynicism'. And what both these examples will show is that Žižek is clearly concerned to keep open the possibility of theorizing an ethics that remains unconstrained by, or which transcends, ideology.

But before entering into a more detailed discussion of these issues or themes, it is necessary that we come back to the ever-important notion of 'the Real'. As I have already clearly indicated, the spectre of 'the Real' looms large in Žižek's ethical theory, and we shall indeed witness how Žižek's ethical privileging of notions such as 'belief' and 'responsibility' only make sense when theorized against the backcloth of 'the Real'. At first sight, then, Žižek's ethical theory seems to draw a certain cogency, consistency or clarity precisely by being grounded in terms of 'the Real'. But things never move so smoothly with Žižek, or, better still, with the notion of 'the Real'. The simple reason for this is that 'the Real' is a paradoxical concept. What does this mean? Up until now, I have focused on the concept of 'the Real' as that which bears witness to the fragility and contestability of meaning in the symbolic-ideological field: 'the Real' of 'antagonism' as I have been calling it. With this, and with Žižek, I have assumed that 'the Real' is a necessary or unavoidable feature of social life through virtue of the fact that it indelibly leaves its destabilizing trace in the symbolic-ideological field. It was in this sense that I referred to 'the Real' as *immanent* to the symbolic and the ideological. Now, what this account of 'the Real' fails to acknowledge is the truly paradoxical twist or sting in Žižek's tale: namely, that 'the Real' is not only a *necessary/ unavoidable* feature of the social-ideological field, but that it is also simultaneously *impossible* to appropriate it adequately within the symbolic realm. Or as Žižek himself puts it:

> The Real . . . is that which cannot be inscribed . . . the rock upon which every formalization stumbles. But it is precisely through this failure that we can in a way encircle, locate the empty place of the Real. In other words, the Real cannot be inscribed, but we can inscribe this impossibility itself, we can locate its place: a traumatic place which causes a series of failures. And Lacan's whole point is that the Real is nothing but this impossibility of its inscription: the Real is . . . a void, an emptiness in a symbolic structure marking some central impossibility.[4]

So how, then, does this notion of 'the Real' as 'impossible' impact on Žižek's ethical theory, and how does it play out in his ethically motivated critique of ideology? For Žižek, we are inevitably caught up in the following paradoxical situation: a) as ethically motivated critics of ideology we are necessarily or unavoidably involved in the symbolic activity of investing meaning in, and thereby privileging, certain ethical norms or values (for example, 'belief', 'responsibility', 'freedom' and so on); b) yet, the idea of symbolically investing an unproblematic or incontestable meaning in such ethical values is something that we perpetually encounter as 'impossible': that is, we inevitably experience a kind of 'failure' or, what Žižek also calls, 'lack' which pervades our symbolization of what we assume to be 'ethical'; c) and this 'failure' or 'lack' manifests itself through virtue of the fact that what we symbolically assume to be 'ethical' is, in the end, continually threatened by the taint, or polluting influence, of ideology.[5]

If all of this sound terribly ambiguous, not to mention potentially confusing, then we can, for the moment, content ourselves with one basic thought, which is this: the critical distinction between the ethical and the ideological offered by Žižek is a rather messy one in that it tries to allow for slippage from one into the other. It is precisely this basic thought or core intuition that we will see played out and, hopefully, rendered more concrete in Žižek's critical evaluation of ethical belief as against the ideology of cynicism, and in his favouring of ethical responsibility over the ideology of totalitarianism. And it is to these themes or issues that we must now direct our specific attention.

Ethical responsibility and the ideology of totalitarianism

In his *Did Somebody Say Totalitarianism?*, Žižek defines 'totalitarianism' as 'a kind of *stopgap*: instead of enabling us to think . . . it relieves us of the duty to think, or even actively *prevents* us from thinking'.[6] Totalitarianism is, and forever remains on Žižek's account, an *ideological* notion in as much as it stultifies thinking, and in so far as it prohibits us from reflexively and critically interrogating the circumstances in which we find ourselves, and our actions within this context. So we immediately see that Žižek's concern with delineating the meaning and significance of totalitarianism is essentially a philosophical or theoretical exercise in trying to clarify the ways in which critical and interrogative thinking is subject to certain ideological constraints. Defined, or analysed in this way, then, 'totalitarianism' as a signifier can assume a very broad feel and resonance within socialpolitical life. Indeed, it is the great merit of Žižek's vast, sweeping analysis that he forces us to confront the operation of totalitarianism in a multiplicity of guises and conjunctions, some of which will no doubt shock and provoke his readers. Consider, for instance, his comparison of the 'New Right populism' of Jorg Haider with 'New Labour'. Žižek writes:

> Haider likes to emphasize the affinity between New Labour and his Austrian Free Democrats, which allegedly renders irrelevant the old Left/Right opposition: they both break with the old ideological ballast, combine a market economy (deregulation, etc.) with the community-based politics of solidarity (help for the old, children, and the socially deprived) – that is, they seek to assert communal solidarity outside the old welfare state dogma.[7]

Žižek's point here is not to say that Tony Blair and Jorg Haider are political soulmates: that is, he explicitly recognizes that Haider's appropriation of Blairite motifs masks a 'xenophobic' populism which is, in a sense, quite foreign to 'New Labour'.[8] Yet, there is, Žižek insists, a deeper connection between Blair and Haider: 'Haider is in fact a kind of uncanny double for Blair, his obscene sneer trailing New Labour's big smile like a shadow.'[9] What does Žižek mean by making this provocative remark? Žižek's claim is this: 'New Right populism' such as that exemplified by Haider trades on, or feeds off, the weaknesses and inconsistencies of liberal-leftist politics. That is to say, 'New Right populism', from a Žižekian perspective, exploits the total lack or absence of radicalism in liberal-leftist political discourse by formulating what the latter strictly prohibits: namely, an 'anti-capitalist rhetoric'.[10] It is precisely here that we touch, Žižek would say, on the 'totalitarian' and expressly 'ideological' nature of liberal-leftist discourse. Put simply, liberal-leftists labour under what Žižek would call the 'hegemony of liberal-democratic capitalism' by essentially conforming to, and never seriously questioning, the economic imperatives that issue from it: for example, the liberal-leftist politician (Žižek explicitly has Blair and Clinton in mind here) would be reluctant to upset the markets too much by raising public expenditure to a level where it would threaten 'capitalist profitability'.[11] In other words, by accepting the economic imperatives of 'global capitalism', we are, in Žižek's terms, effectively relieved of the duty to think, we are ideologically prevented from thinking that change within the economic system, in the sphere of production, is possible: 'it seems easier to imagine the end of the world than a far more modest change in the mode of production' is Žižek's tragicomic way of putting it.[12]

If totalitarianism operates, as Žižek argues, by ideologically relieving us of 'the duty to think', then an obvious way to counter its subjugating force is to engender a form of thinking that is actively critical with respect to ideological orthodoxy and hegemonic opinion. Indeed, Žižek would insist that the subject has a duty, and precisely an ethical or moral duty, to engage in the kind of critical thinking that implicitly and explicitly challenges the ideological status quo. It is important to emphasize the proximity of Žižek to Kant in this respect. By drawing on Kant, Žižek wants to stress the importance of duty as that which gives the subject the opportunity and autonomy to assume responsibility for the ethical or moral norms that they take to guide their actions. By not passively or uncritically accepting the norms and values that shape social life, the subject, on Žižek's Kantian-inspired account, can properly be described as entering the field of ethical responsibility. Žižek argues:

> The unique strength of Kant's ethics lies in . . . [its] formal indeterminacy: moral Law does not tell me *what* my duty is, it merely tells me *that* I should accomplish my duty. That is to say, it is not possible to derive the concrete norms I have to follow in my specific situation from the moral Law itself – *which means that the subject himself has to assume the responsibility of 'translating' the abstract injunction of the moral Law into a series of concrete obligations.* In this precise sense . . . the ethical subject bears full

responsibility for the concrete . . . norms he follows – that is to say, the only guarantor of . . . positive moral norms is the subject's own contingent act of performatively assuming these norms.[13]

There is much in this passage that could detain and intrigue us, and many a follower of Kant's moral and political philosophy would no doubt raise a sceptical eyebrow at Žižek's rather creative suggestion that the Kantian 'moral Law' needs to be interpreted in accordance with a logic of contingency and performativity.[14] For our present purposes, though, it is necessary that we maintain an explicit focus on the notion of ethical responsibility that Žižek here garners from Kant, and how precisely it can be juxtaposed with, what I want to call, the ideology of totalitarianism. And Žižek's position on this issue can be summed up thus: where the ideology of totalitarianism is essentially *instrumentalizing* and *perverse*, ethical responsibility is essentially *inventive* and *hysterical*. Let me develop these points in more detail, taking each in turn. To illustrate the idea that totalitarianism ideologically operates in accordance with a logic that is instrumentalizing and perverse, we can (again to employ a favoured example of Žižek's) refer to the suspect morality of anti-Semitism or 'Nazism'. In Nazism, Žižek argues, we are confronted with a decidedly instrumental and perverse ethical norm or, what he also calls, 'notion of Good': namely, that the removal of the 'Jew' is an ethical act necessary for the establishment of 'a true community of German people'.[15] Now, the instrumental and perverse nature of this norm is, as Žižek points out, clearly reflected in the fact that it is uncritically taken by the 'Nazi' ideologue to override any and all other ethical considerations and obligations: that is to say, the systematic purging of the 'Jew' is instrumentally and perversely accepted as the ethical price to be paid for establishing a true community of German people. Coming back to Kant's ethics, or Žižek's Kantian ethics, it is important to understand this expression of 'Nazi normativity' as nothing less than a refusal to think about, or assume responsibility for, the horrendous consequences that follow from uncritically accepting a norm as self-evidently ethical: this, then, is why Nazism should be considered morally problematic.[16]

With this, we can begin to see how Žižek's Kantian inspired notion of ethical responsibility stands against the kinds of totalitarian ideology that capture subjects by preventing them from thinking critically about the ethical consequences of their actions. For, as we have seen from the passage just quoted, the great lesson of Kantian ethics, the great strength of the notion of ethical responsibility bequeathed to us by Kant, is, Žižek contends, that ethical norms should never be simply and uncritically accepted as such: that is to say, they must be invented every time, on each occasion, by the subject who contingently and performatively assumes responsibility for them. It is in this sense, therefore, that the assumption of ethical responsibility by the subject is essentially an *inventive* act. In what sense, though, is this assumption of ethical responsibility hysterical? The subject of ethical responsibility is a *hysterical* subject, Žižek would argue, to the extent that it resists full integration or acquiescence with regard to moral-ideological orthodoxy: the hysterical subject, in other words, resists 'interpellation' into 'the symbolic' realm of shared norms and moral meanings precisely by positing or inventing new norms and new moral meanings.[17] Yet – and this is an important point for Žižek – the price to be paid for the hysterical and inventive act of positing new norms and moral meanings is that it simultaneously creates uncertainty concerning whether a particular assumption of ethical responsibility, or exercise of duty, is itself possibly tainted by ideology. Or, put more simply and generally, we can think we are acting in a responsible and ethical manner, we can think that our actions are nobly beyond the pathological influence or taint of ideology, when in fact we are pathologically caught in the grip of ideology.[18]

One of the ways in which Žižek illustrates the dangers alluded to above is by imagining the psychological economy of a subject who posits or mobilizes a distinct sense of 'moral duty' as a way of rationalizing the most horrible or horrendous acts. That is to say, Žižek cautions us to be critically aware of the possibility that seemingly normative concepts such as 'duty' can actually provide a convenient mask behind which to hide a pathological desire to engage in, for example, sadistic and violent behaviour. It is worth quoting Žižek at length on this point:

> [W]e need only to recall the proverbial example of a severe sadistic teacher who subjects his pupils to merciless discipline and torture – of course, his excuse to himself (and others) is 'I myself find it hard to exert such pressure on the poor kids, but what can I do? It's my duty!.' The more pertinent example is that of the Stalinist politician who loves mankind, but none the less carries out horrible purges and executions; his heart is breaking while he is doing it, but he cannot help it, it's his duty to the Progress of

> Humanity . . . What we encounter here is [a] properly perverse attitude . . . it's not my responsibility, it's not me who is effectively doing it, I am merely an instrument of the higher Historical Necessity . . . The obscene *jouissance* of this situation is generated by the fact that I conceive of myself as exculpated from what I am doing: isn't it nice to be able to inflict pain on others in the full awareness that I'm not responsible for it . . .[19]

We can see from this passage that Žižek is concerned to track or trace the subjective slide from assuming a certain form of supposedly moral 'duty' to the perverse *'jouissance'* or 'enjoyment' of engaging in sadistic behaviour. And, crucially from Žižek's perspective, this slide from 'duty' to an explicitly 'perverse' sadism can only happen through an ideological displacement of, what I have been calling, ethical responsibility. That is to say, the 'totalitarian' and properly 'perverse' subject (for example, the 'severe sadistic teacher' or 'Stalinist politician') is ideologically prevented from thinking or critically acknowledging the fact s/he is acting in an ethically irresponsible manner. Like the self-professed 'sex addict' who excuses his/her infidelities by blaming a biological affliction over which s/he supposedly can exercise no control, the totalitarian and perverse ideologue will say: 'It was not my fault! I am not responsible! There is nothing I can do!'[20] From Žižek's point of view, the properly ethical response or point here is simple: the severe sadistic teacher, the Stalinist politician and the sex addict *are responsible* for the norms they follow, and, consequently, for the corresponding actions that they engage in. So we see that if the subject is threatened by the perverse and sadistic taint of ideology, then this is only because s/he has been seduced by the obscene *jouissance* or enjoyment that follows from the abandonment or ideological displacement of ethical responsibility. And, says Žižek, it is precisely this abandonment or ideological displacement of ethical responsibility that Kantian ethics strictly 'prohibits'.[21]

It would be unforgivably remiss to end this part of the chapter, as I now must, without acknowledging the essentially precarious, ambiguous and, ultimately, *paradoxical* terms on which Žižek's Kantian ethic of responsibility proceeds. For while Žižek makes great use of a Kantian notion of ethical responsibility to engage in a critique of the perverse, sadistic and instrumentalizing ideology of totalitarianism, he nonetheless is keen to emphasize the potential slippage between the two. In fact, Žižek wants to go so far as to argue that we can never be absolutely sure that our ethical responsibility or duty to the norms we follow is totally free from the kinds of pathological, sadistic and perverse motivations that mark the actions of the totalitarian subject. In this way, the subject remains, as I implied a moment ago, uncertain as to whether their particular assumption of ethical responsibility is tainted by the pathological influence of ideology. As ever, it is important to understand this difficulty against the intuitive backcloth of 'the Real'. Understood in accordance with the paradoxical logic of 'the Real', the notion of ethical responsibility is, in Žižek's terms, both *necessary* and *impossible*. The notion of ethical responsibility is a *necessary* part of our subjective experience precisely because it – Žižek argues after a Kantian fashion – acts as an *unavoidable* limit or condition of our individual freedom. In other words, it is only by following the injunction to do one's duty and assume responsibility for norms that the subject can achieve any kind of critical autonomy or freedom with respect to the values that govern and shape social and ethical life. Yet – and this is equally important – ethical responsibility is simultaneously *impossible* to exercise with absolute certainty. To make, and repeat, the basic point: we can never be absolutely certain as to whether our duty and responsibility to assumed ethical norms is, at least in part, pathologically and ideologically driven.[22]

Ethical belief and the ideology of cynicism

If Žižek's favouring of ethical responsibility over the ideology of totalitarianism is marked by a kind of ambiguity or uncertainty, then this uncertainty is, we shall see, also reflected in his privileging of ethical belief as against the ideology of cynicism. What is less uncertain, what is in fact it perfectly certain, is Žižek's constant concern and desire to critique and expose the ideological function of cynicism or, what he also calls, 'cynical reason'. So how, then, can we account for the ideological operation of 'cynicism' or the practice of 'cynical reason'? Playing on, and developing, a well-known phrase and intuition that he takes from Karl Marx's *Capital*, Žižek defines the ideological operation of cynical reason in accordance with the following formula: 'they know that, in their activity, they are following an illusion, but still, they are doing it'.[23] Three points are worth making in order to clarify Žižek's argument here. First, it is possible, Žižek contends, for us to subject ourselves to an ideology that we consider illusory, and still cynically follow it even in the knowledge that it lacks any truth or validity. So, to take an obvious example, we know that politicians lie, that they are primarily concerned with maintaining a grip on power at all costs, that they engage in 'spin' and tailor facts in accordance with their own interests, and yet we still vote for them, we still listen and scrutinize what they say, we still enjoy the sport of political journalists harassing and exposing them for the liars that we already cynically take them to be. Now this, second, does not mean that we should congratulate ourselves on our sceptical and cynical attitude; that we should enjoy the fact that we do not take seriously the ideological deceptions and lies of politicians. Žižek's claim, and it is a crucial one, is this: beneath the superficially expressed cynical attitude, beneath the enjoyment of cynical critique, we can still act – that is, vote, listen and critically scrutinize political discourse – in a way that materially presupposes that politicians ideally ought to be trustworthy, righteous, concerned with the public good and so on. Our cynical enjoyment, in other words, is materially conditioned by an image of the political that is, in fact, naive and rather idealized. And this is precisely where ideology enters the picture: it is this 'fetishistic illusion' or 'fantasy' that continues to structure our image of 'social reality'. Therefore, and this is our third point, the cynicism adopted apropos the ideological deceptions of politicians is, Žižek insists, not properly critical or subversive: rather, to set ourselves at such a 'cynical distance' is immediately to 'blind ourselves to the structuring power of ideological fantasy'.[24]

So we see that the ideology of cynicism, as we want to call it, is best understood in terms of material practice; in the way that it relates not to what we know, but rather to what we in fact *do*. Now, the question of how ethical belief stands against this ideology of cynicism is, from a Žižekian perspective, a thorny and difficult one precisely because there is a sense in which belief itself can actually function to supplement or support the 'ideological fantasy' sustained by the practice of 'cynical reason'. Indeed, belief and cynicism, Žižek wants to show, can ideologically operate in remarkably similar or analogous ways. We can illustrate this point by drawing on a striking passage from Žižek's *On Belief* where he critically analyses the notion of 'freedom of choice' which, as he says, operates 'at the very nerve centre of liberal ideology'. In contemporary or 'late-capitalist' societies our belief in freedom of choice is, he argues, structured against the background anxiety that we live in, to use a phrase coined by the sociologist Ulrich Beck, a 'risk society'.[25] This creates a political situation in which:

the ruling ideology endeavours to sell us the insecurity caused by the dismantling of the Welfare state as the opportunity for new freedoms: you have to change jobs every year, relying on short-term contracts instead of long-term stable appointments. Why not see it as the liberation from the constraints of a fixed job, as a chance to reinvent yourself again and again, to become aware of and realize hidden potentials of your personality?[26]

Žižek's point here, which is obviously clear from the ironic and caustic terms of his argument, is essentially a simple one: our belief in 'freedom of choice' is ideologically structured in accordance with the 'liberal' fantasy of a late-capitalist 'risk society'. And further, this form of ideological belief has an important cynical aspect. The key thing to bear in mind here is that ideological belief, like cynicism, is best understood as a specific form of material practice: belief is all about the *doing* rather than the knowing. So while we may be superficially cynical about the so-called 'freedom' to choose job insecurity, while we may refuse to believe the ideological suggestion that we are living in a post-welfare-state 'risk society', our actions may still materially presuppose conformity with respect to the imperatives of the market forces of late capitalism. Žižek refers to this form of cynical belief as 'objective'. By this he means that belief has a kind of *thingness* that rather strangely stands outside the consciousness of the subject who acts in accordance with it. Indeed, the ideological belief that we must act in a way that materially presupposes complicity to the economic imperatives that we take to issue from the market forces of late capitalism has, for Žižek, a clear *thing-like* quality: we behave like an unconscious or blind 'automaton' whose involuntary belief is further reinforced by each conformist action or move in the global-capitalist game.[27]

Taken together, notions of belief and cynicism appear to have a clear analogous structure: that is to say, they both can function to blind us, as Žižek would say, 'to the structuring power of ideological fantasy'. And yet, insists Žižek, there is something about belief that stands autonomous from, or indeed transcends, ideology or ideological fantasy: this, of course, is the notion of what we want to call 'ethical belief'. So what, then, does the term 'ethical belief' signify, and how can it be thought to transcend ideology? The Žižekian conception of ethical belief is, as he understands it, a properly Christian one: that is, ethical belief as a form of 'faith'.[28] In a fundamental sense, ethical belief as faith is to be analysed in resolutely political terms, as an 'act' that has clear and direct political significance. This is shown by the fact that Žižek inextricably ties the notions of belief and faith to the concept of the 'event'. As we saw in the last chapter, Žižek develops his concept of the event by drawing closely on the political and ethical philosophy of Alain Badiou. The important point again to bear in mind here is this: by exhibiting a faith in the event, by maintaining a fidelity to the event, the 'subject' becomes politicized by coming to believe that wholesale restructuring of the political sphere is possible; that the state of any given society can be comprehensively disassembled; that the political authority of the state or ruling ideology can be revealed as nothing other than a product of the imaginings of those subject to it. In this way, then, faith and belief in the event is a properly political faith and belief in the possibility of revolution.[29]

If belief as faith is irreducibly political through virtue of having a revolutionary tenor, then on what terms, according to Žižek, can it also be considered ethical? By drawing creatively on the philosophy of Kierkegaard, Žižek wants to argue that the subject becomes ethical only in and through a kind of revolutionary fervour: that is, when the subject truly believes in the possibility of its own 'rebirth', or when the subject truly believes that it is possible 'to start one's life all over again'.[30] What Žižek is saying here about ethical belief dovetails neatly with the concept of subjective destitution that was discussed in the last chapter. That is to say, the revolutionary fervour and force of ethical belief is expressed, as Žižek would say, through a 'withdrawal' from, and '(re)constitution' of, the symbolic field of shared norms and moral meanings. Again we can think back, for illustrative purposes, to Žižek's discussion of the 'mysterious' Keyser Soeze from Bryan Singer's *The Usual Suspects*. Soeze's ethical belief in the necessity of killing his family in order to maintain his freedom from a blackmailing rival mob clearly involves both a withdrawal from, and (re)constitution of, the symbolic realm in which he finds himself. That is to say, by cutting himself loose from 'the symbolic' – that is, the shared space of moral meaning that is the familial network – he is able, on Žižek's provocative reading, to ethically reconstruct or change his circumstances: he is able, in other words, to pursue, and kill, his rivals without the threat of blackmail and without the fear of reprisals.

We can postpone, at least for the moment, any critical comment on the clear moral provocation implied by Žižek's adoption of Soeze as a kind of heroic figure of ethical belief, but we shall see that it is far from an unproblematic notion.[31] It is sufficient, at this juncture, to simply acknowledge that Žižek theorizes the possibility of such a revolutionary and, as he sees it, ethical act by insisting on its autonomy from the forms of ideological fantasy that restrict and constrain the libidinal economy of subjects: ethical belief, like the notion of subjective destitution before it, signifies the possibility of 'traversing the fantasy'.[32] So we can begin to see that the distinction between ideological belief and ethical belief is, from a Žižekian perspective, quite striking and substantive. Where ideological belief is a kind of involuntary or unconscious belief that uncritically reinforces itself through conformist action, ethical belief, properly speaking, involves a conscious and active recasting or, as Žižek would say, 'reinvention' of the self. Where ideological belief cynically blinds us to the structuring power of fantasy, ethical belief, properly speaking, moves beyond or transcends ideological fantasy in providing the subject with the opportunity to be 'reborn' in the kind of faith that allows for the redrawing of the socio-ethical landscape.[33]

This, importantly, though, is not the whole story, and I must conclude this part of the discussion, and indeed this fifth chapter, by coming back to the note of caution with which I began it. Earlier I said that Žižek's privileging of ethical belief over the ideology of cynicism was marked by a kind of ambiguity or uncertainty. The reason for this, as I have already implied and to some extent anticipated, is that Žižek's privileging of ethical belief only takes on its full sense when theorized against the backcloth of 'the Real'. Understood (yet again) in accordance with the paradoxical logic of 'the Real', the notion of ethical belief is, in Žižek's terms, both *necessary* and *impossible*. Ethical belief is a *necessary* part of our subjective experience precisely because it – Žižek argues after a Kierkegaardian fashion – functions as an *unavoidable* condition of our individual autonomy. That is to say, we are only effectively free when we fully and consciously choose to believe in, or have faith in, the possibility of recasting or 'reinventing' the self.[34] Although, and this must equally be borne in mind, ethical belief is simultaneously *impossible* to practise with absolute certainty and consistency. In other words, the subject of ethical belief forever courts the danger of slipping back into ideology. This potential subjective slide from ethical belief into cynical and ideological belief is, Žižek argues, a clear and present danger in our contemporary political culture, not least because the practice of cynical reason is often ethically construed and privileged as something critically subversive and potentially 'liberating'.[35]

It is no doubt fitting that we end our engagement with Žižek's ethics by grappling with the paradoxes of 'the Real'. This, of course, hardly comes as a shock given the importance of this notion to his critical theory or 'critical conception of ideology'. In a sense, Žižek's continual and overwhelming reliance on the notion of 'the Real' already anticipates, to a large extent, the terms on which a critical interrogation of his thought must proceed. I will explicitly formulate a critique of Žižek's related notions of 'the Real' and the ethical in the eighth and concluding chapter by drawing on Habermas and Deleuze. That is to say, we shall see how Žižek's concept of 'the Real', and how his ethical theory, can be interrogated from a Habermasian and Deleuzian perspective. But before I engage in such a cross-comparative and critical analysis, it is necessary to begin to get a sense of how Deleuze's thought, and particularly his ideology theory, sits alongside those of Žižek and Habermas. And this will be a specific concern in the following two chapters.

6 • Deleuze's Ideology Theory

In this chapter and the next I will focus on the work of Gilles Deleuze, teasing out or introducing the ideology theory implied by his thought (chapter 6), before exploring the ethical terms on which a Deleuze-inspired critique of ideology could proceed (chapter 7). By stressing, as I will towards the end of this chapter, that Deleuze is concerned to draw a critical distinction between the ideological and the real, I implicitly and immediately signify a formal homology between his ideology theory and that of Žižek and Habermas discussed in previous chapters. Of course, such a general, but nonetheless important, comparison of Deleuze with Žižek and Habermas says nothing, or very little, about the specificity or particularity of Deleuze's thinking. And it is almost superfluous to say that we should expect Deleuze's critical theory to express a difference which is particular or idiosyncratic. Indeed, we shall see in the first part of the chapter how Deleuze's account of reason significantly departs from that of Habermas and Žižek; and, in the second part of the chapter, how his theory of subjectivity contrasts sharply with, what we can call, the 'humanism' of Habermas. In the third and final part of the chapter I will focus more explicitly on Deleuze's theory of ideology. Better still, we shall see that he is expressly concerned to critically employ the concept of ideology, and that he is motivated by the prospect of engaging in a particular kind of ideology critique. In order to underscore or make sense of this crucial point I will draw on Deleuze's (and Guattari's) critique of the Freudian theory of desire in their path-breaking book *Anti-Oedipus*.

Reason and desire

Despite their undoubted differences in substance and emphasis, both Habermas and Žižek exhibit, what we could call, a faith in the progressive power of reason. This much we have already seen in earlier chapters. In chapter 2 we saw how Habermas insisted on the idea that reason has a universal scope and domain. Or, more particularly, we saw how Habermas theorized the universality of reason as mediated through, what he called, 'communicative action oriented to mutual understanding'. Habermas's argument here, to recap, is that when communicative actors come together in dialogue and debate they always or invariably reason with one another by raising claim and counterclaim in a bid to convince the other of the validity of their view through the sheer 'force of the better argument'. Further, it is best, from a Habermasian perspective, to think of the universal or invariable presence of reason in communicatively mediated social interaction as essentially a progressive and moral force to be critically harnessed against the dangers and debilitating effects of ideology in political life. Indeed, we saw, most particularly in chapter 3, that Habermas's critique of consumerism, scientism/technology and the ideological prejudices of tradition were all implicitly grounded in the intuition that they unreasonably or irrationally violate our moral sense.

If Habermas's advocacy of the use of reason in social and political life is unambiguously or categorically affirmative, then in Žižek we find a notion of rationality that is altogether more ambivalent and problematic.[1] This is because Žižek insists, as we saw, on understanding the status, scope and function of reason by theorizing it against the background of an exploration of 'fantasy'. In essence, Žižek wants to argue that fantasy can condition reason, and can crucially shape and affect how reason is used in the social world. In this regard, fantasy can work, as Žižek would say, to 'plague' or 'blur' reasoning in a way that can have morally problematic and ideologically regressive consequences. Consider again, for example, Žižek's analysis and ideology critique of 'anti-Semitism'. As we saw in chapters 4 and 5, anti-Semitism or 'anti-Semitic paranoia' is a form of fantasy-plagued reason which projects an image of 'social reality' – a notion of the 'social bond' that is pathologically threatened by the figure of the 'Jew' – that is criticizable, Žižek insists, on the grounds that it fails to come to terms with the genuine sources of conflict and 'antagonism' in social life. With this ideology critique of anti-Semitism, of course, Žižek offers us the prospect of a reasoned critique of reason, or a negative critique of one form of fantasy-plagued reasoning that implicitly assumes a more rational way of looking at the social world. So we have seen that although Žižek is keen on treating the notion of reason in a problematical fashion, he nonetheless insists on the progressive possibility of a more or less rational critique of the fantasy-images or fantasy-projections upon which ideology so ceaselessly trades and functions.

Understood against the backdrop of this Habermasian and Žižekian faith in the progressive power of reason, Deleuze's thought could appear altogether curious, something of an oddity. For Deleuze does not especially show any faith in reason, and, at certain points, openly exhibits hostility to the notion. In a highly influential and provocative work, *Nietzsche and Philosophy*, Deleuze draws on the thought of Friedrich Nietzsche in order to critically interrogate the idea that we can never, properly speaking, assume a certain faith in reason precisely because reason is itself always something created, posited anew, perpetually reconstructed and imbued with different values.[2] So, from a Deleuzian perspective, the critical question to ask is not whether we should have faith in reason; rather, we ought to be asking how the notion of reason originated and assumed significance and value in the first instance. In trying to answer this question it would be unforgivable, Deleuze suggests, to overlook or underestimate the important and significant role played by Kant. In Deleuze's eyes, Kant is a 'genius' or a truly revolutionary figure in the history of philosophy or human thought because he insists on imbuing the notion of reason with a properly *critical* significance or value.[3] What does this mean? Two points are worth bearing in mind here from a Kantian perspective. First, the use of reason has a critical value or significance in the obvious sense that it is immediately tied to the activity of critique or criticism. And, second, the activity of critique that is mediated through the use of reason has value in a strictly moral sense because it signifies the exercise of individual autonomy and the birth of, what Kant calls, 'enlightenment'. As Kant himself puts it in his essay 'What is enlightenment?':

> Enlightenment is man's release from his self-incurred tutelage. Tutelage is man's inability to make use of his understanding without direction from another. Self-incurred is this tutelage when its cause lies not in lack of reason but in lack of resolution and courage to use it without direction from another. *Sapere aude!* 'Have the courage to use your own reason'! – that is the motto of the enlightenment.[4]

Kant's point, then, is that 'enlightenment' proceeds from an individual's courage to use their 'reason' and direct their 'understanding' in an autonomous and critical fashion: that is, 'without direction from another'. Without this critical use of reason, Kant caustically argues, there can be no genuine freedom in thought, in fact no thinking at all: 'If I have a book which understands for me, a pastor who has a conscience for me, a physician who decides my diet . . . I need not trouble myself. I need not think . . . others will readily undertake the irksome work for me.'[5] So we can see from Kant's remarks that he is concerned to posit or stage an inextricable or irreducible link between the concepts of reason and critique: that is to say, he understands the use of reason as the motor which drives the activity of criticism.[6] While acknowledging the novelty and influence of Kant's argument that critique is mediated through, or conditioned by, the use of reason, Deleuze nonetheless believes it to be inherently problematic. Deleuze's challenge to the Kantian notion of reason can be summed up thus: by insisting on the idea that critique is mediated through, and conditioned by, the use of reason, Kant must effectively assume a kind of faith in reason itself as that which is beyond criticism. And Deleuze's point in response is that reason as a concept must be subject to criticism, to the kind of critical evaluation that traces how it is created, posited, perpetually reconstructed and imbued with different and shifting values. Following Nietzsche, Deleuze refers to this mode of critical evaluation as 'genealogy'.[7]

While there is much provocation and much of interest in Deleuze's Nietzschean or 'genealogical' critique of Kant, it is sufficient, for our purposes here, to insist on a point of more general significance: namely, that a Deleuze-inspired critique of the notion of reason must be characterized by a focus on the mode of its creation, and on the way it assumes value in social and political life.[8] And the question of how reason operates and assumes value in social and political life is, as I will show, one that can be illuminated through a discussion of Deleuze's concept of *desire*. Indeed, by theorizing the notion of reason against the backcloth of a Deleuzian concept of desire, we can see how the former becomes problematic through virtue of being mediated through the latter. Put simply, we shall see that Deleuze's insistence on the presence and mediating influence of desire in social life implies a critique of reason. In order to make sense of this intuition it is necessary to draw on one of Deleuze's most well-known and infamous works, *Anti-Oedipus*. Written with his long-time collaborator and friend Félix Guattari, *Anti-Oedipus* is a veritable tour de force that has as its aim the construction of a concept of desire that is unencumbered by what they see as the difficulties and deficiencies of psychoanalysis.[9] What, then, characterizes this non-psychoanalytical or, what Deleuze and Guattari actually call, 'schizoanalytical' conception of desire? The first thing we should take cognizance of is that Deleuze-Guattarian desire is defined as something inherently *positive*. In stark contrast to the traditional psychoanalytical model that understands desire as a reactive response to an unsatisfied want or lost object, Deleuze and Guattari insist that desire is active, that it functions in social life by producing connections in, what they would call, a 'machinic' fashion. In the opening sentences of *Anti-Oedipus*, Deleuze and Guattari describe this machinic operation of desire thus:

> It is at work everywhere, functioning smoothly at times, and other times in fits and starts. It breathes, it heats, it eats. It shits and fucks . . . Everywhere it is machines – real ones, not figurative ones: machines driving other machines, machines being driven by other machines, with all the necessary couplings and connections. An organ-machine is plugged into an energy source machine: the one produces a flow that the other interrupts. The breast is a machine that produces milk, and the mouth a machine coupled to it . . .[10]

What are we to make of Deleuze and Guattari's remarks here? Two important points are worth bearing in mind in this context. First, by insisting that desire operates in a machinic fashion they claim to be making a literal rather than 'figurative' or metaphorical statement: desire, as they see it, literally functions by way of machinic connection and production. Second, the operation of desire is not, from a Deleuze-Guattarian perspective, something that can be adequately analysed with exclusive reference to individual psychology: desire, as they see it, is essentially impersonal or de-individuated, but it can nonetheless affect individuals or subjects in interesting ways. Let us try to make better sense of these, admittedly difficult, points by animating them through a concrete example. Consider, for instance, the way a filmmaker uses a camera to create a vision or perception of something that would normally escape the human eye. Think about the well-known (often documentary) camera technique of rendering perceptible instances of motion or events that would ordinarily remain imperceptible to our everyday human gaze: for example, the opening of a flower or the daily work of a community of tiny ants. What we have here, from Deleuze's perspective, is a machinic operation of desire whereby one machine (the human eye) literally functions or connects with another machine (the inhuman eye of the camera) in order to create or produce something new: namely, a modification in the field of human perception (the rendering perceptible of the opening flower or community of ants). Or, put slightly differently, the human eye of the individual confronts the impersonal eye or, what Deleuze would call, 'superhuman eye' of the camera with the effect that it changes and assumes a new focus or capability.[11]

So what, we may be forgiven for asking, do these ruminations concerning the machinic operation of desire have to do with the notion of reason? Or, more particularly, how does Deleuze's insistence on the presence and mediating influence of desire in social life imply, as I suggested a moment ago, a critique of reason? In a basic sense, reason is, from a Deleuzian point of view, a product of desire. Or, put another way, the social reality that we reason in, or reason about, is produced and mediated through the fixation or structuring of desire, and must be critically understood as such.[12] In *Anti-Oedipus*, Deleuze and Guattari focus their attention on a critique of a particular type of reasoning: that is, they provide a critique of psychoanalytical reason. One of the core intuitions at play in Deleuze and Guattari's critique of psychoanalytical reason is that they consider it to be a repressive force in social and political life, reflecting, as they say, the 'wants', 'needs' or values of 'the dominant class' in the contemporary 'market economy'.[13] Deleuze and Guattari's claim is this: by fixating or making desire operate around the notion of 'lack', by implying that desire is a reactive response to an unsatisfied want or persistently lacking object, psychoanalysis provides the perfect *raison d'être* for capitalist consumption and production. Psychoanalytical reason, in other words, literally teaches us to desire by instilling in us the fear and anxiety that our 'wants' and 'needs' are not yet satisfied, and this, Deleuze and Guattari insist, is nothing but a ruse to generate, on behalf of the 'dominant' capitalist class, ever more economic production and consumption.[14]

Subjectivity and difference

As we have just seen, Deleuze's conception or notion of desire is marked by an insistence that it be analysed from a 'machinic' point of view of production and connection: we need, from a Deleuzian perspective, to critically account for the movement of desire, or the way desire creates a certain movement in the order of things (again we could think of the example of the 'superhuman' eye of the camera and its effect on reorganizing human perception). In a sense, we could say that this expresses Deleuze's vitalism, where 'vitalism' signifies an enduring intellectual concern or curiosity in the process of change or transformation.[15] It is against the backcloth of Deleuze's vitalism that we need to theorize his conception of subjectivity. Simply put, Deleuze's notion of subjectivity is thoroughly vitalist in orientation in that he constantly tries to think subjectivity as a process or, as he would say, as a 'struggle' for the 'right to difference, variation and metamorphosis'.[16] So we see that there is a strong sense in which Deleuze's vitalist approach to subjectivity is inextricably linked to the problem or issue of difference. Let us immediately be clear on this important point: by seemingly attaching significance to the subjective struggle for the right to difference, Deleuze is not simply advocating the kind of liberal individualism or 'humanism' that understands the difference of the subject in terms of an autonomous right to maintain a unique, irreplaceable and inalienable sense of self. In this regard, Deleuze's theory of subjectivity contrasts sharply with the kind of humanism we find in Habermas, for instance, where the subject's uniqueness and autonomy are said to be built into the very fabric or structure of communicative action. Against this form of humanism, Deleuze wants to argue that the subject, or what we consider to be 'human', is not unique, irreplaceable and inalienable, but is rather fragile, contingent and malleable. In other words, Deleuze wants to claim that subjectivity cannot simply be understood in terms of a set of predetermined or ascribed characteristics of the 'human' (that is, uniqueness, autonomy etc.) precisely because the difference at play in the structure of subjectivity means that the human is constantly caught up in a process of change and mutation.[17]

Deleuze's stress on the malleability of the 'human', on the difference at play in the structure of subjectivity, is a constant refrain which echoes through all his writing and thought. From his earliest books on the history of philosophy to his later collaborative work with Félix Guattari, Deleuze time and again comes back to this issue. For this reason it would be possible to approach the twin Deleuzian themes of subjectivity and difference from a plurality of angles and with many a shifting emphasis.[18] But we can be content here with a focus on his very first book, published when Deleuze was still in his twenties. Deleuze's *Empiricism and Subjectivity: An Essay on Hume's Theory of Human Nature* is, as the name obviously suggests, a book that focuses on the philosophy of David Hume in order to explore the notion of subjectivity or, what he calls, 'the problem of subjectivity'.[19] Now, this exploration of the structure of subjectivity is immediately theorized by Deleuze in the vitalist terms that we have already indicated above. 'The subject', he asserts, 'is defined by the movement through which it is developed.'[20] One way of coming to terms with the vitality and difference of the subject would be to critically acknowledge its creative power or capacity to establish what Deleuze, following Hume, calls 'relations' between 'ideas'. What Deleuze is suggesting here, among other things, is the possibility that a subject is capable of performatively engaging with ideas, of staging relations between ideas, in a way that produces a constitutive change or transformation in the structure of their subjectivity.[21]

So how, then, are we to understand the process whereby the subject engages with ideas, or stages relations between ideas, so as to constitute a movement or change in the structure of their subjectivity? In order to make sense of this question, it will prove useful to detour a little by shifting our attention to Deleuze's work on cinema, specifically his *Cinema 1: The Movement-Image*. For it is in this work, a book written some three decades after *Empiricism and Subjectivity*, that Deleuze again puts to work his Humean theory of 'relations' to illuminating and concrete effect. We can see this, for instance, in his engaging treatment of the work of Alfred Hitchcock, and in his particular analysis of Hitchcock's 1948 film *Rope*.[22] Before beginning to understand how a Deleuzian analysis of *Rope* can help us render more concrete his theory of subjectivity, it is necessary that I initially give a very brief narrative outline of the film. Seduced by the idea of 'committing the perfect murder', Brandon Shaw and Phillip Morgan invite a mutual acquaintance and former classmate David Kentley to their apartment with the clear intention of strangling him. After killing Kentley and hiding his body in a chest in their apartment, they wait, anxiously and excitedly, for the mutual friends and family of the deceased to arrive for a pre-arranged dinner party. Kentley's family and friends arrive, wonder where he is while they unsuspectingly eat from the chest-come-buffet-table in which he lies dead. Yet, as the night progresses one of their dinner party guests, their former school master Rupert Cadell, comes to suspect foul play and, in the end, he confronts and challenges his former pupils to account for the missing Kentley . . .

From Deleuze's perspective, Hitchcockian films such as *Rope* provide us with a clear expression of, what he calls, the 'fabric of relations' through which the subject actively constitutes and reconstructs itself.[23]

Let us, by way of illustrative example, focus on who is undoubtedly the key figure or character of the film: Brandon Shaw. Shaw is animated by a clear will to dominate others, or by a tendency to manipulate, cajole and impose himself on those he believes to be inferior to him. Positively drunk on the pseudo-Nietzschean idea that he is 'culturally superior' to the 'ordinary man', that this cultural superiority elevates him above and beyond the ordinariness of traditional moral concepts such as 'good' and 'evil', he considers himself both intellectually and aesthetically justified in killing a supposedly 'inferior being' such as David Kentley. 'The Davids of this world', Shaw explains in a justificatory and hyperbolic speech to his accomplice, 'merely occupy space, which is why he was the perfect victim for the perfect murder.' Unable to constrain his excitement and exhilaration, he continues:

> I have always wished for more artistic talent, well murder can be an art too. The power to kill can be just as satisfying as the power to create. Phillip, do you realize we have actually done it, exactly as we planned, and not a single infinitesimal thing has gone wrong. It was perfect . . .
> We've killed for the sake of danger and for the sake of killing. We're alive, truly and wonderfully alive . . .

Turning back to Deleuze's Humean conception of subjectivity, we can clearly see that Shaw is engaged in a performative and excessively theatrical staging of a 'relation' between certain 'ideas' that are constitutively crucial to his developing sense of self. Most immediately, we see that Shaw's intellectual and aesthetic justification of Kentley's killing involves staging an essentially hierarchical relation: that is, the relation of 'superior' to 'inferior' being. This relation or theme is interestingly and cleverly animated throughout the film, being subject to much multiplication, twisting and turning. We see it clearly in Shaw's pompously superior disdain for the supposed vacuity, tedium and fastidiousness of his dinner guests. In Janet Walker, David Kentley's fiancée, Shaw finds an excessive vacuity and insincerity. Believing Janet's romantic attachment to David to be essentially meaningless, or driven solely by a desire for his money, Shaw invites her old boyfriend, and former best friend of David's, Kenneth Lawrence to the party. The acute embarrassment caused by this rather malicious staging of events is, for Shaw, the obvious source of a rather perverse comic amusement. In Mrs Attwater, David's paternal aunt, Shaw finds a tedious and rather stupid figure. Indeed, Shaw's contempt for Mrs Attwater is so thinly veiled, his belief in her stupidity so settled and certain, that he directly censors and mocks what she says without any concern that she may respond in kind. In Mr Kentley, David's father, Shaw finds an essentially fastidious, morally conservative and unimaginative man.

Shaw's resentment toward David's father is brought into sharp focus in a particular scene where he, Mr Kentley and Rupert Cadell engage in a debate about the aesthetics and morality of murder. By insisting that murder can be considered an 'art' practised by 'superior individuals' on 'inferior' victims, Cadell provokes Kentley to respond and raise the obvious question as to how anybody could reasonably or morally justify such a provocative view. Shaw weighs into the discussion in order to provide a rationale for the assertions of his former teacher. Employing, as we earlier put it, a pseudo-Nietzschean notion of 'cultural and intellectual superiority' Shaw, with a progressive intensity and violence, explicitly denounces Kentley's faith in social and moral convention, insisting that it expresses a clear failing of 'intelligence' and 'imagination'.

So we see that the 'fabric of relations' through which Shaw actively constitutes his sense of self implies a particular staging of himself as 'culturally superior' to the murdered Kentley and his family and friends. Yet the pseudo-Nietzschean imaginings of Shaw become altogether more problematic when we come to think about the relation that develops between him and Rupert Cadell. Shaw considers Cadell to be an intellectual equal and, as their debate with Mr Kentley seems to show, similarly committed to a supposedly Nietzschean aesthetic of murder. In a way, Cadell acts as a kind of mouthpiece for Shaw, providing for him a form of intellectual encouragement to articulate, justify and rationalize the murderous act that he has engaged in. But this, we see, is not the whole story as the relation between Shaw and Cadell sharpens around a central antagonism which provides the dramatic backdrop to the conclusion of the film. Ashamed and traumatized by the realization that his former pupil has used his pseudo-Nietzschean ideas to justify murder, Cadell seeks to sever any relation with Shaw by exposing his lack of humanity as something fundamentally foreign to him. Or, as he explicitly puts it in his final remarks to Shaw:

> Tonight you have made me ashamed of every concept I ever had of superior or inferior beings. But I thank you for that shame. Because now I know that we're each of us a separate human being . . . with a right to live and work

and think as individuals, but with an obligation to the society we live in. By what right do you dare say there is a superior few to which you belong? By what right did you dare decide that [David Kentley] . . . was inferior and could therefore be killed? Did you think you were God, Brandon? Is that what you thought when you choked the life out of him? Is that what you thought when you served food from his grave? . . .

If Cadell's denunciation of Shaw here unsatisfactorily borders on the melodramatic, then this is clearly because it is seemingly predicated on a rather theatrical and sensational conversion to the kind of humanism that previously seemed so unappealing to him. And yet such a melodramatic scene is, at least from a Deleuzian perspective, useful or productive in the sense that it animates the notion of a Hitchcockian 'relation' and a mode of subjectivity undergoing dramatic change, or even termination.[24] That is to say, we witness a dramatic shift or change occurring between Cadell and Shaw in the obvious sense that the former seeks to remove any intellectual or aesthetic justification for the latter's murderous act. Or, put another way, the hierarchical relation that Shaw tries to stage between 'superior' and 'inferior' beings, and his corresponding sense of self as 'culturally superior', literally seems to collapse under the progressive weight of the caustic and thought-provoking questions thrown at him by Cadell. That these caustic and thought-provoking questions – 'By what right do you dare say there is a superior few to which you belong?' . . . 'Did you think you were God, Brandon? Is that what you thought when you choked the life out of him?' – come to express a vital and profound force is clearly shown by Shaw's response to them. For he says nothing; no longer is he inclined to argue; no longer does he express a will to intellectually justify his actions; no longer does he exhibit a will to dominate; no longer does he seem to be aesthetically seduced by the idea of his own murderous power and creativity. In short, Shaw is shamed into silence.

From a Deleuzian point of view, the 'shame' that Shaw feels, that Cadell makes him feel, is significant because it implies a critique of the former's narcissistic love of power. Everything here pivots around a proper or adequate understanding of Shaw's Nietzscheanism or pseudo-Nietzscheanism, as I have rightly been calling it. The reference to Nietzsche throughout *Rope*, and Shaw's explicit reliance on the Nietzschean concept of the 'superman', are, as Deleuze might say, almost 'cartoon-like' in their provocation and simplicity.[25] Shaw is, in

Deleuze's terms, a 'cartoon superman' in the sense that he expresses a will to dominate or exert power over others: his is a will 'that wants power'.[26] This we have already seen expressed, most dramatically, in Shaw's belief that the power to kill the 'inferior' other is at once aesthetically creative and life-affirming. Further, the will to power or will to dominate expressed by Shaw is thoroughly narcissistic in the obvious sense that it originates from a particular individual's self-absorbed and self-aggrandizing assumption of 'superiority'. Against Shaw's individualizing and narcissistic appropriation of the Nietzschean 'superman', Deleuze critically insists on understanding the latter in an impersonal or depersonalizing way. From Deleuze's perspective, the 'superman' is not simply represented by the actions or will of a powerful or dominant figure, but is, rather, best thought of in terms of a process whereby the subject changes or becomes different through virtue of encountering something forceful and disturbing outside itself. And this, we should note, is precisely what is dramatized in the final scene of *Rope* when we witness how Cadell's forceful arguments against Shaw act as so many depersonalizing hammer blows that come from the outside to rob the latter of his culturally superior sense of self.[27]

If the Deleuze-inspired analysis of *Rope* I have engaged here is useful in helping us come to terms with his vitalist conception of subjectivity, then this is because it brings into focus three important intuitions that must now be made explicit. First, the difference at play in the structure of subjectivity implies, for Deleuze, a kind of performativity on the part of the subject who can experiment with 'ideas' in order to fashion or develop a particular sense of the self (for example, Shaw's staging of himself as culturally superior to the murdered Kentley and his family and friends). Yet, and this is the second point, the sense of self performatively assumed by the subject is, Deleuze would argue, constitutively fragile because it can be disturbed and essentially depersonalized by forces that are outside it (for example, the forceful arguments of Cadell which effectively disturb and destroy Shaw's sense of self). And third, and perhaps most importantly, the performative assumption of self-identity is also, Deleuze insists, ethically criticizable if it is predicated on a particular subject's narcissistic love of power and, as in the case of Shaw, on a will to dominate. In generalizing or broadening this crucial third point we could say that Deleuze is concerned to engage in a critical evaluation of the particular modes of subjectivity that he finds ethically problematic: that is to say, base, unworthy, contemptible or shameful. Of course, to conclude this part of the chapter, as I now must, by merely emphasizing that there is a discernible ethic at work in Deleuze's theory of the subject is a clear form of provocation. Immediately we are moved to ask: what kind of ethics does Deleuze offer in the face of the base, unworthy, contemptible or shameful? I will focus explicitly on the issue of Deleuze's ethics in the next chapter. For the moment, though, we need to turn our attention to Deleuze's concept of ideology, or, more specifically, to introducing the kind of ideology theory that is implied by his thought.

The real and the ideological

The first thing that we should acknowledge concerning Deleuze's understanding of the concept of ideology is that he seems, at least at first sight, to express an open hostility concerning its critical utility. That is to say, he seems, at certain points, to express (in a manner that was strikingly similar to his friend and philosophical contemporary Michel Foucault) a scepticism concerning the efficacy or value of the notion.[28] For example, in their delightfully baroque and hugely influential work *A Thousand Plateaus*, Deleuze and Guattari categorically announce: 'There is no ideology and never has been.'[29] In light of such sceptical remarks it may seem strange to insist that there is a 'critical conception of ideology' to be taken from Deleuze, or, more particularly, that Deleuze can help us draw a distinction between the ideological and the real. The irony or paradoxical nature of such an enterprise would not be lost on the critics, commentators or Deleuze scholars who take him at his word, assuming he is simply unconcerned with the issue of ideology.[30] However, and as shall be shown, things are not quite as cut and dried as they may first appear. By drawing briefly on his, and Guattari's, critique of the Freudian theory of desire in *Anti-Oedipus*, we will see that Deleuze is expressly concerned to critically employ the concept of ideology. That is to say, Deleuze and Guattari engage in an ideology critique of Oedipus, or, more particularly, the 'oedipal' or 'oedipalizing' logic that they take to be inherent in the Freudian notion of desire. Put simply and somewhat more generally, what I want to begin to suggest, in this final part of the chapter, is that Deleuze provides us with a critical sense of what it means to flee or take flight from the constraining influence of the ideological.[31]

Let us begin, then, by looking briefly at how Deleuze and Guattari critically assess the oedipal or oedipalizing logic that they take to be inherent in the Freudian notion of desire. What issues are at stake here? Simply put, and as is well known, Freud believed that the continuing narrative power and resonance of the Greek tragedy of Oedipus was reflected in the fact that it articulated or staged what is essentially a universal or fundamental, albeit repressed, human desire. For Deleuze and Guattari, Freud's categorical mistake here is to assume that desire can be forever explained as a timeless and unconscious replaying of an oedipal drama (or 'Oedipus complex'). Against this image of unconscious desire as a 'theatre' for 'representing' Oedipus, Deleuze and Guattari insist that the unconscious is best thought of as a 'factory': that is, a site for the real production or the creation of desire.[32] So, Deleuze and Guattari's point is that Freud mistakenly sees the oedipal drama as 'representing' a universal image of desire, rather than, as they would see it, producing or creating a specific image of desire. The supposedly 'universal' drama of Oedipus does not explain or provide a foundation for understanding the nature or origin of desire. On the contrary, the appearance and use of the oedipal drama is something that must be explained or critically accounted for. As Deleuze and Guattari put it in a crucial passage:

> Only in appearance is Oedipus a beginning, either as a historical or prehistorical origin, or as a structural foundation. In reality it is a completely ideological beginning, for the sake of ideology. Oedipus is always and solely an aggregate of destination fabricated to meet the requirements of an aggregate of departure constituted by a social formation.[33]

The significance of this passage – at least for our purposes – is obviously reflected in the fact that Deleuze and Guattari mobilize or use the concept of *ideology* to critically account for the 'fabricated' or constructed nature of Oedipus. What this clearly implies, of course, is that the concept of ideology still retains a specific critical purpose and utility in helping them come to terms with the way desire is constituted in psychoanalytical discourse. Two general points are worth emphasizing in order to finesse and clarify the notion of ideology that Deleuze and Guattari are critically employing here. First, if ideology refers to the 'fabricated' nature of social phenomenon such as the 'oedipalization' of desire, then a critique of this ideology obviously implies bringing into sharp focus its constructedness. In this sense, ideology critique implies, what Deleuze and Guattari would call, a constructivism, where 'constructivism' signifies a critical sensitivity to how supposedly universal, eternal or timeless concepts (that is, 'Oedipus complex', 'reason', 'subjectivity' and so on) are, in reality, the product of specific fabrications or creations.[34] Now, this does not mean that the operation of ideology in social life is simply a matter of trickery, whereby the dominant elite convince the duped masses of a lie which represses their interests and ensures their continuing servitude. Rather, ideology also works through the structuring or fixation of desire, and the ideologically repressed, Deleuze and Guattari provocatively conclude, *remain in servitude precisely because they have been literally moved to desire it.*[35] In a sense, this was the crucial point of Deleuze and Guattari's suggestion that psychoanalytical reason teaches and moves us to desire what we supposedly 'lack', thereby providing the perfect *raison d'être* – or, as we can now put it, ideological justification – for desiring ever more capitalist consumption and production.

The second important point which needs to be emphasized is that Deleuze and Guattari explicitly ground their ideology critique (of Oedipus and the Freudian theory of desire) with reference to the concept of 'reality'. Does this not suggest the possibility that, in our terms, a critical distinction can be drawn between the ideological and the real? Of course, before we can broach this question we need to clarify what precisely the term 'reality' signifies in this context. Deleuze and Guattari are quite categorical on this issue, and are worth quoting accordingly:

> There is no such thing as the social production of reality on the one hand, and a desiring-production that is mere fantasy on the other . . . The truth of the matter is that *social production is purely and simply desiring-production itself under determinate conditions.* We maintain that the social field is immediately invested by desire, that it is the historically determined product of desire . . . *There is only desire and the social, and nothing else.*[36]

By insisting that desire functions to produce the social field, or by emphasizing the productive co-existence of desire and the social field, Deleuze and Guattari provide what they would consider to be a vitalist conception of social reality; remembering that, for Deleuze and Guattari, desire itself is thoroughly vitalistic, defined as it is by machinic production and connection, by movement, openness and change. Desire is not something necessarily sedimented, fixed or constraining, but it can be structured as such if we are moved slavishly to desire in a certain way. In a sense, this is precisely where ideology enters the picture, where it begins to work its questionable magic. Again we can consider, by way of illustrative example, the actions of Brandon Shaw in *Rope*. If Shaw is to be critically rebuked as a pseudo-Nietzschean ideologue, if we are able to subject his actions to a Deleuze-inspired ideology critique, then this is simply because we can show how he was moved to follow slavishly a fixed or constraining form of desire. As we have seen, Shaw expresses a desire to dominate, manipulate, cajole and impose himself on those he believes to be inferior to him. Seduced by the essentially ideological image of himself as a culturally superior 'superman', he fails to recognize this as his expressed and specific desire, a desire that is as challengeable as it is 'fabricated' or constructed. In the end, of course, this ideology critique of Shaw's fixed or constraining desire (that is, his pseudo-Nietzschean 'will to power') is performed by Rupert Cadell whose forceful arguments act as so many hammer blows which effectively destroy the former's 'culturally superior' sense of self. In the Deleuzian terms used above, Cadell's ideology critique bears witness to the 'constructivism' inherent in, or immanent to, Shaw's specifically constituted desire.

Let me conclude this sixth chapter by re-emphasizing a few significant points about the Deleuze-inspired theory of ideology I have begun to bring into focus. First, a critical conception of ideology or critical understanding of how ideology operates in the social field must, from a Deleuzian perspective, proceed from an analysis of its function in constituting, and shaping, desire: that is to say, the critic of ideology must be sensitive to the ways in which subjects are moved to follow slavishly a fixed and constraining form of desire (for example, Brandon Shaw's pseudo-Nietzschean 'will to power'). Second, Deleuze grounds his critique of the 'fabricated' or constructed nature of ideology (for example, the ideology of Oedipus) in terms of a specific notion of 'reality': that is to say, a vitalist conception of social reality which emphasizes the productive coexistence of desire and the social field. This, third, brings us to the distinction between the ideological and the real. In an important sense, 'the real', understood in Deleuzian terms, is a non-ideological or, more accurately, pre-ideological site, expressing the essential constructedness of the forms of desire which influence how we invest meaning in the social world.[37] Ideology enters the picture, and works its questionable magic, only when we begin to assume that these forms of desire are not constructed and open to reconstruction; when we dogmatically, instrumentally and narcissistically fixate on 'our' desire as if it somehow had a transcendent and overriding priority (again we could think of Shaw here). Therefore, and fourth, to take flight from the constraining influence of ideology involves, from a Deleuzian point of view, continually emphasizing the real malleability of desire, and, consequently, the real openness of the social field to change and mutation. Framed or introduced against the backcloth of these four general points, Deleuze's theory of ideology undoubtedly has a rather abstract and sparse feel, and it will obviously prove useful if we can explore it further, hopefully making it a little more concrete as we go. This will be the aim in the next chapter, where I will be concerned to tease out the ethics implied by his critique of ideology.

7 • Deleuze's Ethical Critique of Ideology

In the previous chapter I set about introducing a Deleuzian or Deleuze-inspired theory of ideology. And, as we saw, a number of general points or issues emerged from this discussion, two of which are immediately worth re-emphasizing and further exploring here. The first point concerns Deleuze's stress that ideology operates in the social world through the structuring or fixation of desire, and that the ideologically repressed remain in servitude precisely because they have been literally moved to desire it (for example, the desire for capitalistic consumption to fulfil fabricated 'wants', or Brandon Shaw's pseudo-Nietzschean desire for 'superiority'). And the second point or issue relates to the Deleuzian suggestion that a critique of ideology, that taking flight from the constraining influence of the ideological, involves continually emphasizing the malleability of desire, and, consequently, the openness of the social field to change and mutation. Coming back to the first point, we could shift its meaning slightly by saying that desire becomes fixated, becomes ideologically fixated as such, precisely by being repressed or subject to repression. The core Deleuzian intuition, then, would be this: ideology functions through the repression of desire or, better still, through the desire for repression. I will introduce this important notion in the first part of this chapter by way of a brief discussion of Deleuze's critique of, what he calls, 'control societies'. Now, if Deleuze helps us, as I will argue he does, to detect in control societies a certain ideological desire for repression, then does he also give us any hint concerning how desire may be freed from such repression? This brings us back to our second point: namely, the stress on the malleability of desire in taking flight from the influence of ideology. As we shall see in the second and concluding parts of the chapter, Deleuze does provide us with a way of further underscoring the malleability of desire or, more particularly, how substantive shifts and movements in a subject's desire can imply a critical move beyond the constraints of ideology. What shall become apparent here is the distinct sense that Deleuze is engaged in developing a 'critical conception of ideology' that proceeds on certain ethical grounds: that he offers us an ethical critique of ideology.

Control societies and ideology

Deleuze's 'Postscript on control societies' is an incredibly short piece of writing, running to no more than a few pages. Nonetheless, it is a provocative, rather enigmatic essay; an argument packed with suggestive comments, and interesting allusions.[1] The central contention that Deleuze advances is that late twentieth-century and, by implication, early twenty-first-century society is moving from a 'disciplinary' model to one of 'control'. What does he mean by this? Consider the following passage:

> The key thing is that we're at the beginning of something new. In the *prison system*: the attempt to find 'alternatives' to custody, at least for minor offences, and the use of electronic tagging to force offenders to stay at home between certain hours. In the *school system*: forms of continuous assessment, the impact of continuing education in schools, and the related move away from any research in universities, 'business' being brought into education at every level. In the *hospital system*: the new medicine 'without doctors' that identifies potential cases and subjects at risk and is nothing to do with any progress toward individualizing treatment . . . In the *business system*: new ways of manipulating money, products, and people, no longer channelled through the old factory system. This is a fairly limited range of examples, but enough to convey what it means to talk about institutions breaking down: the widespread progressive introduction of a new system of domination . . .[2]

In general terms, we see the way in which Deleuze is keen to stress the breakdown of essentially disciplinary social institutions – that is, prisons, schools, hospitals, factories etc. – and their mutation in accordance with a particular logic of control. In disciplinary societies individuals pass through social institutions, from one institution to another, constantly finding themselves in the position of having to start afresh. 'Individuals' as Deleuze says, 'are always going from one closed site to another . . . first of all the family, then school ("you're not at home, you know"), then the barracks ("you're not at school, you know"), then the factory . . .' However, in 'control societies you never finish anything'.[3] That is to say, in societies of control, we, for example, never really leave education; we never really exorcize the spectre of the need for, or want of, 'educational retraining' to equip us in a supposedly 'ever-changing marketplace'. As Deleuze puts it: 'many . . . people have a strange craving to be "motivated", they're always asking for special courses and continuing education: it's their job to discover whose ends these serve.'[4] What Deleuze wants to critically, and rather caustically, emphasize here – in a manner that is discernibly analogous to Žižek – is that the assumed desire for 'continuing education' or continual retraining to equip us in a supposedly 'ever-changing marketplace' materially conforms to the controlling tendencies that emanate from the social-political institutions of late twentieth-century and early twenty-first-century capitalism.[5] Or, to generalize the point somewhat: in 'control societies' we are moved ideologically to desire our own servitude, to crave our own repression, in as much as we come to desire the need to be 'flexible' and 'responsive' to the economic imperatives that issue from, what Deleuze calls, 'the instrument of control' that is 'capitalism'.[6]

If Deleuze helps us to detect in control societies a discernible ideological desire for servitude (that is, a desire to conform to the economic imperatives of capitalism), then he also simultaneously gives us a hint concerning how desire may be freed from such repression. Such a critique of ideological repression is undoubtedly alluded to above when Deleuze cautions his readers to be critically sensitive to the 'ends' or interests ideologically served by the fixation, or inculcation, of certain forms of desire. Yet, we need to ask, is this critique an ethical critique in any substantive sense of the term? Or, put more generally, is there an ethics at play in Deleuze's critical theory? The first thing that should be stressed is that Deleuze's *œuvre* is marked by a constant concern to explore the status and scope of the ethical, and that there would be much to detain us if we were to provide a comprehensive survey of the ethical implications of his work.[7] But we can content ourselves here by again drawing inspiration from his work on cinema, in particular his book *Cinema 2: The Time-Image*, and short essay, 'Having an idea in cinema'.[8] What can be extrapolated from Deleuze's cinema work in this context is an image of the subject that is caught up in, what we could call, a *struggle to desire*. By this I mean the process through which any given subject experiences or undergoes a substantive shift in the economy of their desire. Deleuze would want to argue that this process can have a clear ethical import to the extent that it liberates the subject from repressed desire, or from the ideological desire for repression. In this way, the desiring subject is able to ethically move beyond ideology, experiencing the 'liberty' or, what Deleuze would also call, the 'joy' of moving beyond a repressed and repressing desire. Before beginning to make fuller sense of this

Deleuzian image of an ethical critique of ideology, his ethics of joy as I will call it, it is important to have a better grasp of the 'struggle' through which it is said to be mediated.

The struggle to desire

In 'Having an idea in cinema', and, more extensively still, in *Cinema 2: The Time-Image*, Deleuze is keen to stress the ethical and political importance of film. Film, as 'a work of art', insists Deleuze, retains an ethical and political significance to the extent that it is anchored in the practice of, what he calls, 'human struggle'. Deleuze poses the question: 'What relation is there between human struggle and the work of art?' And he answers:

> It is the strictest and for me the most mysterious relation. Precisely what Paul Klee wanted to say when he said: 'You know, the people are missing'... The people are missing: that means that this fundamental affinity between a work of art and a people who do not yet exist is not, and never will be, clear. There is no work of art that does not appeal to a people who do not yet exist.[9]

What Deleuze wants to emphasize here, among other things, is that cinema becomes political, or potentially politicizing, by expressing or showing how the people 'are missing'.[10] What does he mean by this? Well, by making an appeal 'to a people who do not yet exist', political film-makers do not seek so much to represent 'the people' as actually create or invent a new image of 'the people'. Put simply, political cinema, or 'modern political cinema' as Deleuze would say, is concerned not with 'representation', but with the production of new forms of subjectivity.[11] In this sense, and with a backward glance to Deleuze's theory of subjectivity discussed in chapter 6, we could say that 'modern political cinema' plugs into the vitalism inherent in the structure of subjectivity: that is to say, the openness of the subject to the kind of change precipitated by a shift in the economy of desire. To initiate such a shift or change in the economy of desire is never simply an easy matter of choice, but is, in the Deleuzian terms above, always a matter of 'human struggle'. Let me try to make more concrete this image of the subject struggling to shift or change the economy of their desire by drawing on Paul Thomas Anderson's thought-provoking film

Magnolia (1999). We can focus, more immediately, on one of the principal characters in the film: namely, 'quiz kid Donnie Smith'. It may be tempting, at least initially, to think of Donnie Smith as a rather sad, even tragic, figure. An intellectually gifted child made fleetingly famous by his record-breaking exploits on a television game show, Donnie, as a grown man, seems alienated or curiously at odds with the world in which he finds himself. Donnie, we learn, is a man living with the legacy of parental abuse/exploitation (his parents, he tells us, exploited his fleeting celebrity for their own selfish economic gain); a man facing a financially uncertain future (considered incompetent, he is sacked by his boss); a man that seems both confused and disturbed by his own desire. 'I really do have love to give', he says in a telling turn of phrase, 'I just don't know where to put it.'

The shifting movements that give shape to Donnie's desire are animated captivatingly by Thomas Anderson in a particularly moving scene that is worth dwelling on. Here we find Donnie at a bar, assuming a gaze that is fixed, transfixed we could say, on a specific object of desire: namely, 'Brad' the bartender. To underscore Donnie's fascination with his object of desire, Thomas Anderson uses a perceptually subjective point-of-view shot, capturing in slow motion the figure of Brad through Donnie's eyes.[12] What this also reveals is that Brad is wearing braces on his teeth. Why is this revelation significant? For this, at least in Donnie's mind, materially expresses the connection between the two men, and explains why Donnie has invested his time, energy and money in getting braces of his own; why he has followed a course of 'corrective oral surgery'. Suddenly, we are moved to realize that Donnie's desire is to produce or create a connection between him and Brad, a point clearly reinforced by the fact that his gaze at the mouth of the other (Brad) is simultaneously accompanied by the delicate touching of his own mouth. This movement of Donnie's desire, his desire to connect to Brad, is made narratively explicit when he confronts Brad directly, expressing his 'love' by way of a seemingly confused and disjointed monologue. It is worth quoting a fragment of this monologue here:

> I love you, I love you. I'm sick . . . I'll talk to you, I'll talk to you tomorrow. I'm getting corrective oral surgery tomorrow, for my teeth.
> I love you Brad, Brad the bartender. You wanna love me, I'll be good to you. I'll be God damn good for you . . .

How can we make sense of this fragment of strange, and somewhat strained, monologue? Leaving aside Deleuze for the moment, we could argue for a psychoanalytically informed interpretation, *à la* Žižek for instance, which stresses the 'fetishistic split' at play in Donnie's desire for Brad.[13] What this means is that although Donnie effectively knows that Brad has no love for him (the scene makes clear that Brad has no idea who Donnie is, being visibly stunned and disturbed by the latter's impromptu declaration of affection), he chooses to believe in it nonetheless. This, of course, is where the fetishized object (that is, Brad's braces) comes into play. In a sense, Brad's braces come to signify the possibility of a connection between them; that is, the possibility of a love or desire reciprocated. Therefore, from a psychoanalytical perspective, when Donnie proclaims 'I'm getting corrective oral surgery tomorrow, for my teeth', he is expressing a belief in a form of connectedness or reciprocity that he simultaneously knows to be impossible. Further, we could suggest that Donnie's recognition of the impossibility of Brad's love is precisely what makes the monologue of the former so disjointed, so repressed, so self-evidently anxious and disturbed. We see that Donnie expresses his desire ('I love you') only to immediately censor and repress it ('I'm sick'). This to and fro of expressed and repressed desire, of desire released and desire blocked, is emphasized cinematically by Thomas Anderson in a readily discernible way. That is to say, he uses the movement of a whip pan (that is, an extremely fast pan creating a sidewise blurring motion across the screen) to animate Donnie's physical movement toward Brad. This functions as a perceptually subjective point-of-view shot capturing not only the 'spur of the moment' release of desire, but also the vertigo, giddiness, or even nausea, which endures in it (a point graphically reinforced by the fact that we are shown Donnie being physically sick the moment he leaves the bar).[14]

The difficulty with this kind of psychoanalytical interpretation, in Deleuze's view, is its tendency to fixate or focus too much on the repression or blockage of desire. As we saw in the last chapter, Deleuze is concerned to stress what he takes to be the inherent *positivity* of desire: desire is primarily, or primordially, productive or connective in nature and tendency. In this way, Donnie's desire to create and maintain a connection with Brad must be understood first and foremost as a positive and productive act, even if it is consequently marked by failure. The issue, then, for Deleuze would be this: whether or not Donnie consequently succeeds or fails in connecting to Brad, he has already made a move that conditions the possibility for a successful or failed bid for his affections. In other words, before desire is blocked (by way of Brad's lack of recognition), there is a flow or movement that conditions and makes it possible (expressed through Donnie's move to his strained monologue). We can go even further by suggesting that Donnie's movement toward Brad can be thought of as an expression of liberty, where 'liberty' expresses, as Deleuze would say, an 'intensification', an 'elevation of power' and 'a gain in distinction' in the subject who desires.[15] What this means is that Donnie experiences the intensification of his own desire through the rejection of self-censorship or repression; through the expressive power of declaration ('I love you'). This, to be sure, precipitates a feeling of giddiness, sickness even, but – and this is an important Deleuzian point worth repeating – it is also accompanied by a certain 'gain in distinction' in the desiring subject. In this way, Donnie is able, at least in part, to experience the liberty or the joy of moving beyond a repressed and repressing desire.

If we come back to the filmic text we can see the fascinating and increasingly complicated way in which Thomas Anderson explores the joy that is expressed through the character of Donnie. In the first instance we may be tempted to think of Donnie's joy as uncomplicatedly sentimental or trite, as a rather facile mask behind which he tries to hide his sadness. For instance, in a dialogue in the bar we find him making a number of remarks (for example, 'I'll make my dreams come true') that are immediately and caustically dismissed by the fellow drinker with whom he is engaging. In a way, the mocking irony or acerbic wit of this figure acts as a clear counterpoint to Donnie's seemingly facile sentimentalism. Donnie's sentimentalism is also seemingly underlined or underscored by the fact that wherever he goes in his car he is accompanied by the same mawkish pop song: Gabrielle's Dreams. Yet – and this is where things become more complicated – there is something about Donnie's candour and openness, sentimental as it is, that allows him to affect others and be affected by others; that allows him the essentially joyful experience of redeeming himself in the understanding of others. It is virtually impossible to underestimate the importance of the scene in which Thomas Anderson has Donnie, and several of the other principal characters in the film, singing along contemplatively to the Amiee Mann song 'Wise Up'. The poignancy of this scene – which shows different characters at different locations, in different states of consciousness and unconsciousness, simultaneously and collectively engaged in the same act – is partly reflected in the fact that it is anchored in sentimentalism, but a powerful rather than mawkish sentimentalism that signifies not only an affecting connection between seemingly disparate individuals, but also, and perhaps more importantly, the idea that joy in redemption is possible through engaging or acting in concert with others.[16]

The intuition that the 'Wise Up' scene is, at least in part, about joy or the redemptive power of genuinely empathetic relations is followed up by Thomas Anderson as *Magnolia* moves toward its climax. Maintaining our particular focus on the Donnie character, we see that he chances upon an important and rewarding encounter with Jim, a local cop. In a particularly moving scene Donnie confesses to Jim his feelings and retrospective thoughts apropos his desire for Brad. As he says:

> I know I did a stupid thing, so stupid . . . getting braces. I thought he would . . . love me, getting braces. For what? For something I don't even . . . I don't know where to put things, you know. I really do have love to give, I just don't know where to put it.

The tenderness of this scene is ensured by Jim's essentially empathetic response to Donnie's (again rather confused and disjointed) musings. From the point of view of knowledge and events, Jim can understand very little, if anything, of what is being said to him. However, the sentiment of regret expressed by Donnie, or Donnie's internalized belief in his own foolishness ('I know I did a stupid thing, so stupid . . .') resonates strongly with him. In this way, and contra the bar scene with Brad, Donnie's words here have the strength and the vitality to genuinely affect Jim. It is in this sense that Donnie's candour, openness and honesty allow him the joyful experience of redeeming himself in the understanding of the other. To underscore this connectedness Thomas Anderson ends Donnie's monologue by cutting to a close-up of Jim whose considered and sympathetic sigh confirms that the words of the former echo in the previous experiences of the latter. This is something that is also reinforced by the narrative structure of the film. In an earlier scene, for instance, we find Jim scrambling around in search of a gun that was lost during the course of pursuing a suspected criminal. The effect that this has on Jim is striking because it, as he explicitly says in a later scene, merely confirms his worst fears concerning his own ineptitude and foolishness. So we see that both Donnie and Jim are seduced by a rather tragic image of themselves, that they have both internalized a belief in their own foolishness and carry with them a sentiment of regret concerning their past actions. And we see, to repeat the basic point, that Donnie's encounter with Jim is a redemptive one for him as he finds in the other a sympathetic or empathetic ear.[17]

Desire, ideology and ethics

Let us come back to Deleuze. As I have said, the whole point of engaging with Thomas Anderson's *Magnolia*, and the Donnie Smith character in particular, was to animate the Deleuzian idea that a productive shift in the economy of the desiring subject is never a simple or easy matter; that it is always a 'struggle'. Donnie is clearly engaged in a *struggle to desire*. At his worst, Donnie internalizes the pitiable amount of recognition given to him by others (Brad, the parents who exploited him, the boss who sacks him . . .) by pitying himself, by censoring and repressing himself ('I'm sick', 'I'm stupid', 'I used to be smart' . . .). At his best, Donnie refuses to be seduced by this pitiable image of self-contempt, productively using his honesty, candour and openness to carry his desire for understanding and recognition in others (the failed encounter with Brad and the more successful engagement with Jim). In this way, Donnie's struggle to desire swings between two poles: the desire for repression and the desire for a liberty from that which represses. Let me now tie this back to the Deleuze-inspired notion of ideology introduced earlier. Three points are worth emphasizing or re-emphasizing here. First, we could say that Donnie is, from a Deleuzian perspective, gripped by ideology to the extent that he desires his own repression, or to the degree that he wallows in self-contempt and pity. Second, and conversely, we could say that Donnie wrestles free from the grip of this ideology of self-contempt to the extent that he critically rejects the essentially normalizing idea that it should exercise any necessary hold over him. Further, and third, this practical and particular critique of ideology can, Deleuze would insist, be thought of as an ethical critique in so far as it is motivated by a desire for liberty or, what we have also been calling, joy.

To contextualize properly, and thereby understand better, the meaning and significance of this Deleuzian image of an ethical critique of ideology it will prove useful to draw briefly from Deleuze's work on Spinoza. In books such as *Spinoza: Practical Philosophy* and, more extensively still, *Expressionism in Philosophy: Spinoza*, Deleuze develops the notion of an ethics of joy.[18] Put simply, Deleuze's core intuition is this: the desire for joy is at once an ethical desire for the good, where 'the good' signifies the subject's encounter with that which increases its vitality and power. And, conversely, the desire for sadness, or being seduced by a sad or tragic image of oneself, is at once unethical or 'bad' precisely because it signifies weakness and a consequent decrease in the vitality and power of the desiring subject.[19] Understood in these Deleuzian terms, then, the to and fro of Donnie's expressed and repressed desire, his desire released and desire blocked ('I love you', 'I'm sick'), conveys both the play of 'joy' and 'sadness' that is peculiar to him. That is to say, Donnie experiences an ethically unproductive sadness, the diminishing of his vitality and power, when his desire to connect to the other (for example, Brad) is thwarted (again the image of him physically throwing up comes to mind or seems instructive here in conveying this lack of vitality). On the other hand, and as we have seen, he experiences joy, a certain increase in vitality and a gain in distinction, by having the strength to desire and, as in the case of his encounter with Jim, achieve a degree of redemption in the empathetic understanding of the other. It is in this precise Deleuzian sense that Donnie's actions can be critically evaluated in terms of an ethics of joy.[20]

To say that the actions of Donnie as a desiring subject can be evaluated or analysed in accordance with a Deleuzian ethic of joy is not to imply that his joy is only a matter of conscious will or deliberation. Indeed, Deleuze would explicitly and forcefully insist on the idea that the cultivation of joy in an individual can never simply be a personal matter; that the desire for joy is never exclusively the product of the conscious will or intention of the subject. Why is this so? Because desire itself, as we saw Deleuze (and Guattari) argue in chapter 6, operates or is made up of a number of aspects that are essentially impersonal with regard to the individuals or subjects that it nonetheless affects and influences. What Deleuze (and Guattari) want to bring into focus here is the suggestion that desire not only flows from a given individual or subject, but that it also flows through individuals, flows between subjects, in ways that importantly elude their individualizing or instrumental control. Yet again we can rely on the filmic text of *Magnolia* to animate and finesse this idea. Think, for instance, about the 'Wise Up' scene mentioned earlier. As I said, the significance and importance of this scene is reflected in the fact that it signifies not only an affecting connection between seemingly disparate individuals, but also the idea that joy in redemption is possible through engaging or acting in conjunction with others. Now, this expressed desire for joy or redemption in the understanding of the other is one that can be shown, in our Deleuzian terms, to flow through these individuals, moving between them in a partly impersonal, yet thoroughly affecting, way. Before we can begin to make better sense of this claim, it is crucial that we refer to this important moment in *Magnolia* in a bit more detail. Consider the following schematic description or brief segmentation of the scene:

a) Aimee Mann's song 'Wise Up' begins and we find Claudia in her apartment. She is seated: she says, almost inaudibly to herself, 'so stupid' while proceeding to snort cocaine. Then she begins to sing the lyrics of the song, while the camera slowly focuses in on her to the point of a medium-close-up.
b) Then we cut to another apartment, and it is the voice of Jim we encounter in song. The camera slowly pans right to reveal him sitting and singing.
c) Then we cut to the house of Claudia's father, Jimmy Gator. Like Claudia and Jim, he is seated and singing. The camera slowly focuses in on him, but maintains a distance of approximately a medium-long-shot.
d) From Jimmy Gator we cut to Donnie. Seated and singing at his kitchen table, the camera slowly focuses in on him to the point of a medium-close-up.
e) Then we cut to the house of Earl Partridge where he, and his nurse Phil, pick up the song. The camera slowly focuses in on Earl, bypassing Phil as he disappears on the left side of the frame. The camera goes to a close-up of the unconscious and dying Earl. He continues to sing, then stops abruptly.
f) From Earl we move to his wife Linda, whom we find seated in her car. Like Earl, she is unconscious, lifeless apart from the song lyrics that pass her lips. The camera shifts alongside her car moving to a close-up of her head as it rests against the side window.
g) Then we cut to the car of Earl's estranged son Frank. The camera moves from the rear left-hand side of the vehicle, slowly tracking to reveal him in close-up through the side window.
h) Finally, we cut to a close-up of Stanley whom we find seated and singing at a desk covered with books. As with Frank, Claudia, Jim, Jimmy, Donnie, Earl, Phil and Linda, it is only the music and lyrics of Aimee Mann's 'Wise Up' that animate Stanley at this juncture.

Clearly, this brief and sparse outline of the 'Wise Up' scene is meant to be suggestive rather than exhaustive. From a Deleuzian perspective, the important thing to stress is that the music in the scene operates as a kind of mediator through which their desire is collectively expressed. Put simply, each of the principal characters in the scene (Claudia, Jim, Jimmy, Donnie, Stanley, Earl, Phil, Linda and Frank) expresses the desire to, in the words of the song, 'wise up'. What does this mean? As we have already implied, it partly means or signifies that they have come to realize the possibility of redemptive joy in the empathetic understanding of the other. We can reflect on a couple of examples that will give a concrete feel or better understanding of the issues at stake here, at least as they appear from the point of view of a Deleuzian theory of desire. Most immediately, or most familiarly, we can refer once again to the experiences of Donnie. As we have seen, it is in the context of his encounter with Jim that Donnie both consciously desires and explicitly succeeds in garnering some kind of empathetic understanding from the other. Yet, the event that brings Donnie and Jim together, or the circumstance through which the relatively successful movement of Donnie's desire is facilitated, has a *thing-like* independence or decidedly impersonal aspect with regard to the characters involved. What we are talking about here (as those who have seen the film may have already guessed) is what we could call Thomas Anderson's sublimely surprising 'shower of frogs' scene.[21] From this, we see that the meeting of Donnie and Jim is a chance encounter which is conditioned by the fact that they are both caught up in a violent shower of frogs, the latter rescuing the former from the sheer physical onslaught of this freakish storm or turn of events. Now, from the perspective of a Deleuzian theory of desire, this scene is suggestive precisely because it helps animate the idea that the flow of Donnie's desire is not simply a product of his conscious will and deliberation; that it is not merely subject to his individualizing or instrumental control; that desire moves through the social field and social relations in partly impersonal and unconscious ways.

The notion that desire is, at least partly, unconsciously and impersonally conditioned is, to repeat, something already suggested in the 'Wise Up' scene itself. We should note, for example, that both Earl and his wife are singing, expressing their desire to 'wise up', while in a clearly unconscious state (the former suffering from terminal cancer and under the influence of powerful pain-killing drugs, while the latter, seemingly guilt-ridden and depressed, has taken an overdose). While it is tempting to read the use of these seemingly paradoxical images of Earl and his wife as metaphor, to read the music and their singing of it as a metaphorical expression of the unconscious aspect of their desire, it is also important that we recognize how Thomas Anderson literally applies or inscribes the idea that desire is partly unconscious or impersonal into the narrative structure of the filmic text (indeed, the encounter between Jim and Donnie alluded to above already shows this). We can begin to give this notion a slightly different inflection if we take, by way of a second example, the figure of Earl. Earl, we learn, is a dying man whose guilt and regret is the product of the fact that he feels he has failed a previous wife, Lily. Not only did he constantly cheat on her with other women, but he also failed to give her any support or help when she fell seriously ill. Now, the regret Earl feels in relation to his estrangement from Lily is further compounded by the guilt and regret concerning his actions toward their son Frank. This is because Earl ignored and left Frank, who was barely a teenager at the time, with the sole responsibility of taking care of his dying mother. These are circumstances from which Earl desires to 'wise up', and 'wising up' in this context means realizing the possibility of some kind of redemption or joy in reconnecting himself to an alienated son he has not seen in years.

And this is precisely what we glimpse in what is perhaps the most memorable moment of the film. On Earl's request, Phil, his nurse, contacts Frank and he arranges the meeting of father and son. At first the anger, disgust and resentment that Frank expresses towards his father seems implacable. Yet, we quickly see that the callous and cold-hearted nature of Frank's diatribe ('You prick!', 'I hope it hurts', 'She was in a lot of pain', 'I'm not going to cry for you!' . . .) masks the hurt of a son who still cares. 'Don't go way', 'don't go away', becomes the muffled and choked refrain of Frank as he finally breaks down at his father's bedside. At this point, Earl remains unconscious and, consequently, unresponsive to the expressed desire and hope of his son. Yet, it is at this precise juncture that the shower of frogs begins. Crashing violently on the roof and against the windows of the house, the frogs momentarily waken Earl from his drug-induced slumber. Waking to find his son at his side, Earl tries to speak, but cannot. Frank responds to the pathetically feeble movement of his father with a stunned glare, which then gives way to a growing concern. For he recognizes that his father's failed attempts to communicate are seriously draining or sapping the little energy or breath he has left. To help us glimpse Frank's empathy here Thomas Anderson uses a low-angle close-up of him which nonetheless keeps Earl in the bottom right corner of the frame. In this way, the progressively weak exhalations that we see pass Earl's lips function to further animate and connect to the movement and intensification of Frank's concern or anxiety. Read through the lens of a Deleuzian theory of desire, we can see that this scene is important or particularly evocative. For although the brief, and momentarily conscious, encounter between Earl and Frank is an intensely personal affair, it is nonetheless precipitated by an event – the shower of frogs – that is strangely autonomous and independent from their conscious will or deliberation. Therefore, it is in this sense that Earl's desire for empathetic understanding from the other (Frank) is partly unconsciously or impersonally conditioned.

Let me now bring this seventh chapter, and this specific engagement with Deleuze, to a conclusion. Two core points or intuitions emerged and were underscored in the discussions above. First, and most obviously: ideology captures and constrains subjects to the extent that it shapes their libidinal economy. Or, to repeat: ideology functions by way of a repression of desire or, more accurately, through a desire for repression. Now, whether we think about this as a desire for capitalistic consumption to fulfil 'wants', or Brandon Shaw's pseudo-Nietzschean desire for 'superiority', or Donnie Smith's desire to wallow in self-contempt and pity, the Deleuzian point in each case is the same: namely, that the movement of desire has ceased and has become fixated in a way that belies its own constructedness and vitality. Second, and against this image of an ideologically constrained subject, Deleuze offers us the possibility of an ethical critique of ideology; or an image of the subject struggling to desire in a way that moves beyond the constraining influence of the ideological. And it was against this Deleuzian backcloth that I most particularly analysed the movements of Donnie Smith's desire: that I detected, after a certain Spinozian fashion, an ethics of joy at play in his desire to connect to the other (Brad or Jim). Of course, a Deleuzian ethics of joy such as this is obviously predicated on the essentially Spinozian idea that a desire for joy is a 'good' thing; that it constitutes, properly speaking, an ethical act. This is an intuition that needs further exploration, not to mention critical interrogation. This will become the focus of our attention in the next chapter when I come to critically analyse Deleuze's ethics from both a Habermasian and a Žižekian point of view. And we shall see that this critique of Deleuze's Spinozian ethics can also be mobilized in order to raise certain questions against his notion of desire or, more specifically, to problematize the theory of ideology that necessarily flows from this conception of desire.

8 • Conclusion

The guiding theme or concern of this book has been to raise the possibility of developing a *critical conception of ideology*, where a critical conception of ideology presupposes that a distinction can be made between the ideological and the real, and where the critique of ideology is understood to proceed on ethical or moral grounds. By drawing on the critical theory of Jürgen Habermas, Slavoj Žižek, and Gilles Deleuze I have implicitly and explicitly suggested that it is indeed possible to distinguish the ideological from the real, and that it is important to inflect the notion of a critique of ideology with a clear moral or ethical sense. However, it must be immediately acknowledged that what I have said thus far in this regard has rarely gone beyond explication, beyond merely outlining the possibility of a critical conception of ideology *as a possibility*. In other words, I have not critically interrogated the different theories of ideology taken from Habermas, Žižek and Deleuze, nor have I sought to evaluate critically the broader intuitions that are implied by the critical conception of ideology. This is precisely what I need to do in this eighth and concluding chapter. In the first three parts of the chapter I will engage in a cross-comparative and critical analysis of the Habermasian, Žižekian and Deleuzian theories of ideology previously outlined. And the critical gesture to be made here is to play one thinker against the other in order to problematize each respectively (such that I will mount Habermasian arguments against Deleuze, Deleuzian arguments against Žižek, Žižekian arguments against Habermas, and so on). Two important points will necessarily follow or flow from this discussion. First, the moral or ethical terms on which Habermas's, Deleuze's and Žižek's respective critiques of ideology proceed will, when cross-compared, be rendered contestable and problematic. And second, the ways in which Habermas, Deleuze and Žižek intuitively draw a critical distinction between the real and the ideological will be equally rendered contestable and problematic. The crucial question that this analysis will raise, therefore, concerns whether it is actually possible to defend the basic intuitions of a critical conception of ideology in light of this problematization of Habermasian, Deleuzian and Žižekian thought.

And it is this question that I will grapple with in the fourth and final part of the chapter.

Habermas and Žižek

Let me begin by comparing Habermas and Žižek, or with a brief Habermasian critique of Žižek. A good place to start here is with a critical interrogation of Žižek's ethics. And the reason for this is that Žižek's ethics, and his ethical critique of ideology, seems particularly susceptible to criticism as it is characterized by a kind of ambiguity, fuzziness, or even confusion. Indeed, from a Habermasian perspective, Žižekian ethics suffers precisely because of its rather ambiguous status, from the normative confusion it engenders, and from the lack of critical purpose or bite that necessarily follows such confusion. The normative confusion that plagues Žižek's ethics has its origins in his heavy reliance on a psychoanalytically inflected or Lacanian conception of 'the Real'. That is to say, to ground any understanding of the ethical in conjunction with a concept such as 'the Real' is not possible without lapsing into, what Habermas would call, a 'performative contradiction'.[1] By this it is meant that Žižek advances an ethical critique of ideology while simultaneously, and paradoxically, casting doubt on whether such a critique is possible. We can see this if we come back to the key Žižekian concepts of 'ethical responsibility' and 'ethical belief' discussed in chapter 5. Intuitively theorized against the backcloth of 'the Real', or in conjunction with the paradoxical logic of 'the Real', these concepts are considered both *necessary* and *impossible*. That is to say, while Žižek necessarily makes great use of a Kantian notion of ethical responsibility to engage in a critique of the perverse and instrumentalizing ideology of 'totalitarianism', he simultaneously emphasizes the impossibility of remaining absolutely free from it. And, while he invests meaning in a notion of ethical belief that transcends 'ideological fantasy', Žižek nonetheless stresses the constant danger of slippage between the two. It is in this sense that Žižek's thinking lapses into a performative contradiction; that he raises the possibility of critique only to then characterize it as impossible. And the critical question, at least from a Habermasian perspective, is this: how can Žižek sustain an ethical critique of ideology if the very ethical terms on which he proceeds are potentially tainted by the ideological?

CONCLUSION

The claim that Žižek's ethics is tainted by ideology is something that seems explicitly reinforced by his adoption and ethical affirmation of Keyser Soeze as a kind of heroic and radically autonomous figure. As we saw in chapters 4 and 5, Soeze is understood by Žižek as a subject who embraces the act of 'subjective destitution', who insists on 'the non-existence of the big Other', who exhibits the courage and belief that allows to him to redraw the ethical landscape in which he finds himself, opening up a space of 'free action'. From a Habermasian point of view, this Žižekian image of the subject is ideological simply because it is normatively deficient and morally irresponsible. That is to say, there is a kind of normatively irresponsible and rather dangerous heroism in Žižekian critique to the extent that the autonomy of the subject (in this case, Soeze) is ethically judged in terms of a wilful and singular resolve, a resolve that is, if we think about it, devoid of any recognizable moral content. A few Habermasian points or intuitions from chapters 2 and 3 are worth re-emphasizing here: most immediately, that the freedom of the subject is never a product of a singular willing; rather the autonomy of the self is always intersubjectively negotiated in symbolically mediated interaction. In other words, the freedom of the subject is recognized and realized only through a form of communicative action where the individual right to assert autonomy in the first person is reciprocally and universally guaranteed. This means that the actions of Soeze (that is, the killings he engages in) are not, contra Žižek, emblematic of a radical and heroic autonomy, but are, properly understood, morally criticizable as a strategic and subject-centred disavowal of the freedom of others.

It is important to acknowledge the broader implications that this Habermasian critique has for Žižek's theory of ideology, and especially the distinction the latter draws between 'the Real' and the ideological. As we saw in chapter 4, 'the Real' is the problematic and paradoxical idea around which all Žižek's thinking crucially turns, providing the intuitive backcloth against which his theory of ideology must be understood. Crucial here, of course, is Žižek's insistence that 'the Real' provides a critical space that can be distinguished and clearly demarcated from 'the symbolic' field in which ideology operates. To repeat the core point, 'the Real' is a space, or as Žižek prefers, 'place' in which we can wrestle free from the grip of ideology: that is, 'the Real' signifies the possibility of gaining a critical distance from the ideological.[2] Clearly, this critical differentiation of 'the Real' from the ideological becomes problematic as soon as we recognize, with

Habermas, that 'the Real' itself cannot be relied on without lapsing into 'performative contradiction'. So the specific charge that can be laid against Žižek's ethical theory can be equally, and more generally, laid against his ideology theory. The basic point, then, is this: Žižek holds out for a critique of ideology grounded in 'the Real', but, in the very act of grounding this critique in accordance with the paradoxical logic of 'the Real', he immediately renders it 'impossible'. So how – to slightly modify or broaden the Habermasian question asked above – can Žižek sustain a critique of ideology when the terms on which it proceeds are always-already caught up in the paradox of 'the Real' as 'impossible'?[3]

How would Žižek respond to such a critique? Well, if the paradoxical logic of 'the Real' leads to a certain confusion or uncertainty (moral or otherwise), then this, Žižek would insist contra Habermas, is something that we simply have to live with. Or, put more categorically, the subject's experience of ideology, and the subject's desire to critique and move beyond ideology, needs to be acknowledged as always-already caught up in paradox. As Žižek puts it: 'The paradox . . . is that the *stepping out of (what we experience as) ideology is the very form of our enslavement to it*.'[4] Significantly, if not unsurprisingly, Žižek detects or discerns this very form of paradox in the ideology theory and critique of Habermas.[5] As we saw in chapters 2 and 3, Habermas's theory and critique of ideology is intuitively guided by his communicative and normative conception of the real. To again repeat the basic Habermasian claim: to invest meaning in our shared social reality we need to engage in a form of communicative action oriented to mutual understanding. That this form of communicative action has a strictly moral or normative content is reflected in the fact that norms such as social reciprocity and individual autonomy are transcendentally built into the fabric of symbolically mediated social interaction. In other words, Habermas wants to stress how such norms are, as he says, 'idealizations' which 'we cannot do without', which are always 'encountered in practice' as part of the conditions that are 'simply constitutive for socio-cultural forms of life'.[6] So Habermas's point is not that we, speech actors, ought to restrain our egoism in the pursuit of a socially reciprocal 'mutual understanding' but, rather, that this is something we always-already do if we are concerned to engage in communicative action at all. Now, in Žižek's view, Habermas's transcendental insistence on the communicative and normative structure of social relations implies a paradoxical logic to the extent that the 'idealizations' of which he speaks – that is, reciprocity, autonomy etc. – already have a paradoxical status. In other words, Habermas's idealizations are, according to Žižek, 'simultaneously denied and laid claim to', and norms such as reciprocity and respect for autonomy are ideally presupposed even 'though we know simultaneously that this cannot be the case'.[7]

So we can begin to see from this that Žižek is concerned to question the status of the normative idealizations that are taken to be at play in communicative action. On the one hand, Habermas must claim for his normative idealizations a transcendental necessity – again, the idea that norms such as reciprocity and a respect for individual autonomy ideally and indelibly shape our communicatively mediated social relations, shape our experiences, shape the way in which we invest meaning in the social world. Yet, simultaneously, he must insist that the status of these normative idealizations be crucially autonomous from experience, that they, in fact, be irreducible to experience. In other words, Habermas cannot simply make a brute empirical claim that communicative action is always or necessarily normatively oriented and conditioned in everyday practice. The reason for this, as Habermas only too acutely realizes, is that everyday practice and experience constantly teaches us that language-games are forever caught in webs of power, that communication often proceeds by way of strategic manoeuvrings and manipulations that have very little, if anything, to do with fostering mutual understanding. So Habermas finds himself defending his normative idealizations by claiming that they shape experience and social relations in a necessary way, while curiously acknowledging that there is nothing necessarily normative or moral about everyday communicative practice. What we have here, to put it more speculatively or abstractly, is a philosophical commitment to transcendence which is immediately or simultaneously undercut by a sociological recognition of the limits of transcendentalism or transcendental arguments.[8] Or, in Žižekian terms, Habermas is caught in the paradoxical position of claiming that his normative idealizations are *necessary* in conditioning experience, while stressing the *impossibility* of theorizing them purely in terms of our everyday experiences of communicatively mediated social interaction.[9]

This Žižekian critique of Habermas's normativism and transcendentalism cuts right to the heart of his ideology theory precisely because it puts a rather serious question mark against the way in which the latter would want to distinguish the real from the ideological. As we saw in chapters 2 and 3, Habermas argues that we can only make sense of the functioning of ideology in social life by understanding it against the communicatively and normatively structured social reality or social relations through which it is transcendentally conditioned. And we saw, ultimately, that the Habermasian distinction between the real and the ideological is philosophically substantive; the former being thought of in terms of a transcendental necessity that is qualitatively different or autonomous from the contingent and parasitic functioning of the latter. Now, coming back to Žižek, or in light of the Žižekian critique above, we can begin to appreciate how potentially problematic this claim clearly is. For if the transcendental necessity that Habermas claims for his normative idealizations – and, more broadly, for his communicative-normative conception of the real – is curiously, and paradoxically, coupled with the sociological recognition that our everyday experience of communicative action need not be normatively constituted at all, that it may in fact be ideologically saturated in webs of power and strategic manoeuvrings and manipulations, then this clearly undercuts the very distinction that he is trying to maintain between the real and the ideological. Put simply, Habermas's communicative and normative concept of the real is not, on this view, transcendentally distinct or autonomous from the ideological; that is, free from the power relations, manoeuvrings and manipulations that are at play in everyday communicative action.[10]

Deleuze and Habermas

By moving from a Žižekian to a broadly Deleuzian critique of Habermas, we can maintain a focus on the problematic status of Habermas's normativism. The critical point, from a Deleuzian perspective, is to show how Habermas's normativism betrays its own status as such. In order to explore this critical suggestion it will prove useful to revisit and reconsider the way Habermas argues for the priority of communicative action. As we saw in chapter 3, Habermas claims that communicative action oriented to mutual understanding is 'the original mode of language use' and that 'the instrumental use of language' or 'strategic action' is parasitic on it. Put simply, all strategic and instrumentalizing action must, contends Habermas, be formulated with a prior attitude to necessary understanding. Of course, the importance of maintaining this distinction for Habermas is primarily normative or moral. Where communicative action has a clear normative or moral content – again, guaranteeing reciprocity and individual autonomy – strategic action is normatively deficient or morally problematic. The normatively deficient or morally problematic status of strategic action is clearly reflected in its ideological function: that is, in the way it operates through the issuing of non-negotiable and demanding imperatives that repress the 'conditions of normative validity' at play in communicative action. So, when – to again use a favoured example of Habermas's – a bank robber thrusts a gun in a bank-teller's face and says 'Hands up!' he is not engaged in communicative action, but is simply issuing an imperative or demand. Now, from a Deleuzian perspective, the distinction that Habermas tries to draw between the inherent normativity of communicative action and the morally problematic imperatives that operate in and through strategic action cannot stand up to closer scrutiny or critical interrogation. The reason for this, according to Deleuze, is that each and every form of language use is grounded by way of imperatives; by the way it demands and forces the compliance of the addressee. As Deleuze and Guattari put it in *A Thousand Plateaus*: 'Language is made not to be believed but to be obeyed, and to compel obedience'.[11]

What Deleuze and Guattari are saying here is that imperatives, mediated through what they call 'order-words', have a function that is 'co-extensive' with language itself.[12] It is important to finesse this intuition a little bit, lest we fall into the trap of caricaturing Deleuze and Guattari's argument. They are obviously not claiming that all forms of language use are explicitly marked by imperatives, orders, or demanding impositions. Rather, they are suggesting that if we look closely at how language operates, how arguments are made and sustained, we can see that they do *implicitly* function by way of imperatives, orders, or demanding impositions.[13] Now, if we take this Deleuze-Guattarian point seriously – that is, if we are prepared to run with the intuition that all speech action is implicitly and inextricably linked to imperatives – then we should expect to find imperatives *implied* by Habermas's own utterances concerning the normative or moral distinction between communicative action and strategic action. That is to say, we should be able to look at actual arguments and statements made by Habermas in order to critically reconstruct the imperatives that are *implied* therein. Can we draw on any tangible evidence in the hope of making good on this suggestion? The following statement or argument, taken from Habermas's *Moral Consciousness and Communicative Action*, is worth our attention in this respect:

> Individuals acquire and sustain their identity by appropriating traditions, belonging to social groups, and taking part in socializing interaction. That is why they, as individuals, have a choice between communicative action and strategic action only in an abstract sense, i.e., in individual cases. They do not have the option of a long-term absence from contexts of action oriented toward reaching an understanding. That would mean regressing to the monadic isolation of strategic action, or schizophrenia and suicide. In the long run such absence is self-destructive.[14]

The main thrust of this passage should be familiar enough to us by now: strategic action – and the imperatives or orders so characteristic of this form of language use – is clearly thought to be parasitic on 'action oriented toward reaching an understanding'. We can see that this conceptual move is based on a very strong claim concerning the role that communicative action plays in the formation of subjectivity or self-hood. Indeed, Habermas goes as far as to suggest that it is impossible for a subject to consistently engage in strategic action because this implicitly involves an abstraction from the 'socializing interaction' through which it is individuated. What makes this claim interesting and provocative from a Deleuzian perspective is that it does indeed seem to imply an imperative or order. For when Habermas claims that we speech actors 'do not have the option of a long-term absence from contexts of action oriented toward reaching an understanding', that this 'would mean regressing to the monadic isolation of strategic action, or schizophrenia and suicide', he seems to be clearly issuing an imperative. Now, even though this argument or claim is not marked by an explicit threat or demand, it nonetheless implies the following imperative or order: 'engage in the form of communicative action that I am advocating or risk becoming a schizo or suicidal!' In this way, Habermas is arguing for a normative or moral distinction between communicative action and strategic action in a fundamentally non-normative or non-moral way. That is to say, he is not engaged in a reflexively open discussion or debate; he is, to put it rather colloquially, literally telling us that this is the way things are. Therefore, it is in this Deleuzian sense that Habermas's normativism betrays its own status; that his conceptualization of the normative is cognitively grounded in terms of an essentially non-normative or non-moral imperative.[15] In problematizing Habermas's normativism in this way, Deleuze's critique inevitably resonates with the Žižekian critique mapped out above. That is to say, we can begin to see that there are clear Deleuzian reasons for scrutinizing Habermas's theory of ideology, or, more particularly, for calling into question the Habermasian distinction between the real and the ideological. Like Žižek, Deleuze would want to question the supposed transcendental autonomy of the normative from the ideological. Read through a Deleuzian lens, Habermasian normativism – and, more fundamentally, his normative and communicative conception of the real – is actually cognitively grounded on terms that Habermas would himself consider decidedly ideological: that is, on the basis of a non-normative or non-negotiable imperative.[16]

How would Habermas respond to such a critique? Put simply, he would stoutly defend the normativity immanent to communicative action and outrightly reject the Deleuzian suggestion that language use is necessarily or inevitably grounded by way of morally problematic imperatives. We can make sense of this critical response by refocusing on Habermas's rationalism; that is, on his communicative and postmetaphysical conception of reason. As we saw in chapter 2, Habermas insists on the idea that reason is expressed or mediated through language use, that a form of rationality is structurally built into communicative action. When speech actors come together in debate and dialogue they, according to Habermas, invariably reason with one another by raising claims and making arguments which seek to convince others of the efficacy of their view, and they can only legitimately win others around to their view by convincing them through the 'sheer force of the better argument'. In this regard, communicative action or language use is rationally motivated to the extent that it seeks to foster a reasoned agreement or an intersubjective recognition of the 'better argument'. From a Habermasian perspective, Deleuze's own intuition or argument that all speech action is implicitly and inextricably linked to imperatives rather ironically testifies to the immanent rationality of language use. In other words, Deleuze is engaged in a debate or dialogue with his readers – he is advancing an argument which he must necessarily assume as 'better', as worthy of intersubjective recognition or assent. This, of course, is ironic precisely because of Deleuze's hostility to the very notion of reason or rationality. For, as we saw in chapter 6, Deleuze – contra both Habermas and Žižek – shows no particular faith in the progressive power of reason, using Nietzsche to question its utility and significance. So we see that it is precisely this Nietzschean disregard or critical rejection of reason that needs to be questioned and critically interrogated from a Habermasian point of view. Or, as Habermas would say, we need to be critically sensitive to the fact that Deleuze's critique of reason lapses into 'performative contradiction' as it is advanced on the basis of communicatively articulated reasons. And how, asks Habermas, can we have a coherent Deleuzian or Nietzschean critique of reason when such a critique can only be mediated through a process of rational argumentation?[17]

So how, we may ask, does Habermas's critique of Deleuze's Nietzschean rejection of reason connect up with his defence of normativity? Habermas's core intuition is this: to stress the rationality of communicative action is immediately to defend its normativity, as the latter is necessarily implied by the former. In other words, if we can say, as Habermas maintains, that symbolically mediated interaction is rationally structured, then we must assume that it has a precise normative content. This can be shown by the fact that rationally motivated argument or discourse is inescapably grounded on a normative basis; that an intersubjective consensus or agreement concerning the 'better argument' can only be gained when all speech actors party to the dialogical exchange are reciprocally recognized as having the right to assert their autonomous view in the first person. Of course, this Habermasian defence of the normative against Deleuze's critique itself implies a critique of the latter, and precisely a normative or moral critique. In order to see this we need only reconsider Deleuze's ethics or, more specifically, the ethical critique of ideology that was extrapolated from him. As we saw in chapter 7, Deleuze is concerned to critique the forms of ideology that capture and constrain the libidinal economy of subjects. Ideology, to repeat the essential point, functions by way of a repression of desire or, better still, through a desire for repression. Against this image of an ideologically constrained subject, Deleuze offers the possibility of an ethical critique of ideology; or an image of the subject struggling to desire in a way that moves beyond the constraining influence of the ideological. Key here, of course, is Deleuze's Spinozism, and his stress on the ways a subject can desire essentially joyous encounters which increase its vitality and power (recall, for example, the earlier analysis of the figure or character of Donnie Smith from Paul Thomas Anderson's *Magnolia*). Now, from a Habermasian perspective, the implications that follow from this kind of ethical theorizing are morally or normatively problematic in a clear and obvious sense. Deleuze's Spinozian ethics, his ethics of joy, proceeds with the assumption or idea that a desire for joy is a good thing; that it constitutes, properly speaking, an ethical act. But what, Habermas would want to ask, is necessarily good about advocating an ethics of joy, especially when this is predicated on the assumption of power and on the increased vitality of the subject who desires? Or to pose the question rhetorically on Habermas's behalf: is Deleuze simply offering us another version of the Nietzschean will to power, a will to power that irresponsibly and ideologically disregards the communicative relations in and through which moral problems need to be posed and resolved?[18]

The wider implications of this critique of Deleuze's Spinozian ethics can be clearly brought into view as soon as we acknowledge that it poses serious questions concerning his theory of desire. Or, more specifically, the theory of ideology, and the distinction between the real and the ideological, that necessarily flows from Deleuze's conception of desire immediately become problematic as soon as we seek to critically interrogate, after a Habermasian fashion, its morally problematic status. In chapter 6, I introduced the idea that a Deleuzian conception of the real, where the 'real' signifies the productive coexistence of 'desire' and the 'social field', is distinct from the forms of ideology that truncate and repress desire. That is to say, I suggested that ideology enters into the social world, and works its questionable magic, only when we begin to assume that certain forms of desire are not constructed and open to reconstruction; when we dogmatically, instrumentally and narcissistically fixate on 'our' desire as if it somehow had a transcendent and overriding priority (recall, for example, the earlier analysis of the figure or character of Brandon Shaw from Hitchcock's *Rope*). And yet, the very Deleuzian distinction between the real and the ideological becomes impossible to maintain if we insist, with Habermas, that Deleuze's notion of desire is itself constituted on the basis of an ideology of power accumulation, where the desire for increased vitality in the subject is ethically privileged without any real consideration of the moral consequences that follow from this. The inference to be taken from Habermas's critical reproach here can be summed up thus: if the real is productively mediated through the fixation or structuring of desire, or if the real is inevitably shaped by the forms of desire that influence how we assign meaning to the social world, and if these forms of desire operate in accordance with an ideology of power accumulation, then the Deleuzian distinction between the real and the ideological begins to crumble and inevitably break down. Simply put, the Deleuzian real is, for Habermas, always-already ideological to the extent that it is anchored in an unreconstructed Nietzschean will to power that irresponsibly disregards the social relations in and through which the moral invariably takes shape.[19]

Žižek and Deleuze

Like Habermas, Žižek is sceptical of Deleuze's Spinozism. And this Žižekian critique of Deleuze's Spinozism is equally suggestive since it is also self-consciously theorized as a critique of ideology. That is to say, Žižek considers Deleuze's reliance on Spinoza as ethically problematic and explicitly ideological in its consequences. For instance, in *Tarrying with the Negative*, Žižek detects in Spinoza, and more particularly in the 'inspired argumentation' of a contemporary Spinozist such as Deleuze, a real ambivalence on the question of how we may make ethical judgements concerning the problems that are engendered by 'late capitalism'.[20] Indeed, in a more recent work or book-length study of Deleuze, Žižek goes even further by explicitly suggesting how the former may be thought of as an 'ideologist of late capitalism'. What does Žižek mean by this? In order to make his point Žižek draws on a book review written by Jean-Jacques Lecercle in *Radical Philosophy* entitled 'The pedagogy of philosophy'. In this (rather exquisite and finely written) review Lecercle evokes what he takes to be the critical and anti-capitalist thrust of Deleuze and Guattari's *What is Philosophy?* by imagining a scene of a yuppie on the Paris underground reading the particular work in question. Expecting a primer in philosophy, or a philosophy text-book that will provide some fancy jargon for the next corporate seminar, our yuppie finds a book which attacks the culture of advertising, marketing and public relations; that is, its unhealthy appropriation of philosophy and critical thought. In other words, the yuppie is puzzled by his encounter with, as Lecercle says, a 'book explicitly written against yuppies'.[21] Now, Žižek responds to this imaginary scenario with one of his own; one which emphasizes, contra Lecercle, how our yuppie may respond to Deleuze and Guattari not with puzzlement, but with enthusiasm. What Žižek wants to hint at here, in a manner that is discernibly analogous to Habermas above, is that Deleuze's notion of desire, and by implication his sense of the 'real', is, in some way, complicit with the ideological. Žižek is worth quoting at length in this context:

> What, however, if there is no puzzled look, but enthusiasm, when the yuppie reads about the impersonal imitation of affective intensities beneath the level of meaning ('Yes, this is how I design my publicities!'), or when he reads about exploding the limits of self-contained subjectivity and directly coupling man to a machine ('This reminds me of my son's favourite toy, the action-man that turns into a car!'), or about the need to reinvent oneself permanently, opening oneself up to a multitude of desires that push us to the limit ('Is this not the aim of the virtual sex game I am working on now? . . .'). There are, effectively, features that justify calling Deleuze the ideologist of late capitalism. Is the much celebrated Spinozian *imitatio afecti*, the impersonal circulation of affects bypassing persons, not the very logic of publicity, of video clips and so forth in which what matters is not the message about the product but the intensity of the transmitted affects and perceptions?[22]

How could we respond to this critique from Deleuze's point of view? Two, rather general, Deleuzian points can be made against Žižek here. First, that it is somewhat misplaced to critique Deleuze's Spinozian ethics on the grounds that it fails to answer the question of how we may make ethical judgements concerning the problems that are engendered by late capitalism. And, second, that the Kantian inspired ethic that Žižek adopts to stand against Deleuze's Spinozism is itself problematic. We can take each point in turn. The issue of how we can make ethical judgements apropos the social-ideological field is a particularly thorny and difficult one to negotiate, especially if we choose to do it along Deleuze-Spinozian lines. The simple reason for this is that Deleuze has very little time for the notion of ethical judgement. Or, put more strongly, ethics itself does not proceed by way of judgement, but by the way it poses or creates values that help bring about, what Deleuze calls, 'new modes of existence'. To do ethics in this way is, as Deleuze would say, 'to have done with judgement'. He argues:

> Judgement prevents the emergence of any new mode of existence. For the latter creates itself through its own forces, that is, through the forces it is able to harness, and is valid in and of itself inasmuch as it brings the new combination into existence. Herein, perhaps, lies the secret: to bring into existence and not to judge. If it is so disgusting to judge, it is not because

everything is of equal value, but on the contrary because what has value can be made or distinguished only by defying judgement . . . It is not a question of judging existing beings, but of sensing whether they agree or disagree with us . . .[23]

The Spinozism of this passage clearly stands against the Kantianism of Žižek (and indeed Habermas) in the sense that there is an attempt to displace the notion of judgement and emphasize the ethical possibility of emergent and new modes of existence. Where Žižekian and Habermasian ethics provide us with a normative criteria for judging the morally problematic nature of ideology (for example, as a truncation of the communicative, or as a displacement of responsibility), Deleuze insists, Spinozian style, that ethics involves the constitutive practice of posing new values that empower the subject to engender a different mode of existence (think yet again about the figure of Donnie Smith who precipitates a shift in the economy of desire, liberating himself from the repressed and rather tragic self-image that had hitherto constrained him). It is important to note that Deleuze would not see this as necessarily relativizing moral values in accordance with a pre-determined logic of power accumulation (which is implied by the Habermasian claim that Deleuze is advocating a morally irresponsible will to power), or as reproducing the power position of the ideologically dominant (which is implied by Žižek's claim that Deleuze is an ideologist of late capitalism). Rather, Deleuze wants to suggest that the constitutive practice of posing new values can never be determined in advance of their constitution as such. In this way, 'the good' – the values or norms that we invest meaning and significance in – is not something we use to judge, but is something we find we have actually made in accordance with our desiring it as 'good'.[24] Coming back specifically to Žižek's Kantianism we can begin to see the kind of critique implied by Deleuze's Spinozian approach to theorizing the ethical. From a Deleuzian perspective, Žižek's Kantianism is problematic precisely because it is tied to a logic of judgement, a logic that seeks to determine ethical life in advance according to pre-given normative criteria. The problem here is that we lose sight of the fact that ethics or our sense of the 'good' is never determined in advance of its constitution, and whatever values that are invested with significance and meaning (responsibility, belief, freedom or whatever else) are productively desired as such, rather than being presupposed in the first instance. To put it yet another way, a Kantian ethic such as Žižek's fails to account for the emergence of the values that become constitutively meaningful in social and political life, or for the shifts in values and meanings that become inscribed in the ethical.[25]

The critical conception of ideology

The point of engaging in the cross-comparative analysis above – of playing Habermas, Deleuze and Žižek against one another – was obviously to show or acknowledge how their thinking can be subject to critical interrogation. Two basic, and rather obvious, points are worth reinforcing in light of this discussion. First, the moral or ethical terms on which Habermas's, Deleuze's and Žižek's respective critiques of ideology proceed are, when cross-compared, rendered contestable and problematic. Second, the ways in which Habermas, Deleuze and Žižek intuitively draw a critical distinction between the real and the ideological are revealed to be equally contestable and problematic. Of course, the important concern here is the broader implications that this has for, what I have been calling, the 'critical conception of ideology'.

The crucial question, then, is this: is it possible to defend the basic intuitions of the critical conception of ideology while acknowledging the different, even mutually antagonistic, ways in which they are mapped out in the thought of Habermas, Deleuze and Žižek? I think we can, especially if we are given to understand or theorize these intuitions in a particularly *formal* or *formalistic* way. What does this mean? I will make two broad or formal claims in this context which will, hopefully, help to clarify matters sufficiently. First, I want to argue that a critical conception of ideology or, more concretely, a critique of ideology is actually impossible to mount or maintain without intuitively relying on something like a non-ideological or pre-ideological real. Second, I want to argue that a critique of ideology always, whether acknowledged or not, proceeds on certain moral or ethical grounds. Let me now try to tease out these claims in a bit more detail.

The intuition that it is possible to distinguish the real from the ideological can, I have shown, be clearly extrapolated from the thought of Habermas, Žižek and Deleuze. Whether we think of the real in terms of the communicatively and normatively structured relations through which we invest meaning in the social world (Habermas), or as that which signifies the essential contestability and fragility of the meanings that sustain our shared-symbolic sense of the social world (Žižek), or indeed as the essential constructedness of the forms of desire that influence how we assign meaning to the social world (Deleuze), the basic gesture in each case is quite homologous: namely, that the notion of the real is intuitively theorized as a kind of pre-ideological site on to which ideology is then grafted. Of course, to suggest that Habermas, Deleuze and Žižek intuitively share a concern to distinguish the real from the ideological is to say nothing, or very little, about whether the intuition can be justified as such. Indeed, and as we saw in chapter 1, many a student or theorist of ideology would tend to follow thinkers like Paul Ricoeur or Michael Freeden in directly questioning whether it is at all possible to substantively differentiate the real from the ideological. The basic point, to recap, is this: any clear-cut or substantive distinction drawn between the ideological and the real is problematic to the degree that the former conditions the latter. From this perspective, ideology is critically assumed to be an inescapable or omnipresent condition of the real as it is thought to be always-already embedded in the sense-creating activities of actors who invest meaning in the social world. Or, more concretely, we cannot have or develop a shared sense of the social reality we inhabit without drawing on meanings, assumptions, or ideas that are, in some sense, ideologically pre-constituted or determined. In this way, then, we could think (with Ricoeur and also in light of the cross-comparative analysis undertaken in the previous parts of this chapter) of Habermas's, Deleuze's and Žižek's intuitive belief in a pre-ideological or non-ideological real as decidedly ideological, or as particularly insensitive to the ideological influences or aspects implied therein.[26]

In light of such potential criticism, it is important to *formally* underscore the strength, provocation and merit of the intuition that it is possible to distinguish the real from the ideological. Indeed, it is vital that we respect the difference between this formal intuition and the particular conceptions of the real that are offered by Habermas, Deleuze and Žižek, which may, as we have seen, be susceptible to a particular kind of ideology critique. And if we insist on understanding this intuition formally or emptily, by which I mean as an inescapable animating feature or necessary condition of ideology critique itself, then I think we can proceed with it. The claim, as I have already indicated, can be summed up thus: a critique of ideology is actually impossible to mount or maintain without intuitively relying on something like a non-ideological or pre-ideological real. For if we were simply to accept, with Ricoeur and Freeden for example, that the real is irreducibly ideological, that social reality or the social world in which we invest meaning is ubiquitously ideological, then this would mean that a critique of the nefarious forms of ideology we encounter in social life would be impossible to maintain or practice. Why? A critique of ideology (for example, Habermas's critique of 'consumerism' as outlined in chapters 2 and 3, or Žižek's critique of 'anti-Semitic paranoia' as articulated in chapters 4 and 5) immediately implies that the critic is able to maintain some *real* or genuine distance over the thing criticized (that 'anti-Semitic paranoia' is, in *reality*, displaced 'antagonism', or that consumerism does, in *reality*, stunt the prospect of developing democratic forms of 'communicative action' or 'rational-critical' debate). And it is through this gesture of critically maintaining a distance over the criticized ideology that we intuitively rely on something akin to a pre-ideological or non-ideological notion of the real. It is crucial that we differentiate between how this notion of the 'real' is filled out or actualized in practice by a particular critic of ideology (by Žižek as 'antagonism', by Habermas as 'communicative action', or even by Deleuze as 'desire') and the very fact that this gesture can be formally detected as always-already part and parcel of the activity of ideology critique in the first instance. In a way, we could think of the critique of ideology as a kind of *intuitive call to the real*, where this call to the 'real' signifies the possibility and the necessity of obtaining some critical distance and perspective on the ideology criticized.[27]

Let us now turn to the second basic intuition of the critical conception of ideology. The claim or intuition that a critique of ideology ought to proceed on ethical or moral grounds is far from unproblematic. Of course, we already have a distinct sense of this from the cross-comparative analysis undertaken above. That is to say, we have seen how Žižek's ethics can be problematized from a Habermasian and Deleuzian perspective, how the normativism and transcendentalism implied by Habermas's moral theory is questionable from a Deleuzian and Žižekian point of view, and how sceptical Habermas and Žižek are apropos the Spinozism of Deleuze's ethics. What conclusions can be drawn from this? Clearly, the very contestability and antagonism that pervades the differing theories of the ethical or moral advocated by Habermas, Žižek and Deleuze reflects the inherent contestability of the moral or ethical concepts they employ. Further, and especially in light of our analysis above, we are left wondering whether these supposedly ideology-free moral and ethical concepts (for example, Deleuze's Spinozian notion of the 'good' or Žižek's Kantian idea of 'responsibility') are, in truth, inevitably tainted by the ideological. As we saw in chapter 1, Michael Freeden would certainly want to stress the inherently ideological nature of all supposedly ideology-free moral and political concepts. Freeden's core intuition, to repeat briefly, is this: it is impossible to conceive of a critique of ideology that proceeds purely on moral or ethical grounds precisely because our sense of the moral and ethical is mediated through the use of contestable concepts that are always-already ideological as such. In this way, a moral or ethical critique of ideology will always paradoxically flounder to the extent that it inevitably becomes the 'vehicle', as Freeden might say, for yet another form of ideological thinking.[28]

The implication to be taken from Freeden's analysis is that we must recognize a certain collapsing together of the moral, the ethical and the ideological, and that a sober analysis and critique of moral and ethical theory is only possible when we acknowledge its power as a 'vehicle' for different types of ideological thinking. However, from the point of view of a critical conception of ideology, this conclusion soon runs into difficulties. Why? To effectively reduce all theorizations of the moral and the ethical to forms of ideological thinking necessarily involves an indiscriminate levelling of the former. What this means, therefore, is that we have no way of evaluating the relative value of certain forms of moral or ethical thinking as against others, no way of critically holding to account the forms of ideology that arise from such thinking. Further, the assumption buried in Freeden's analysis that we can engage in a more or less sober analysis and critique of different types of ideological thinking – couched in a multiplicity of moral or ethical vocabularies – implies, despite his protestations to the contrary,[29] a kind of crypto-positivism whereby the student of ideology is expected to analyse and critique different values, norms and ideological forms without committing to any value-preference. The clear problem with this, of course, is that it fails to adequately appreciate that the act of engaging in the critical analysis of ideology (or socio-political formations more generally) is itself a value-oriented activity. That critique, and that the critique of ideology more particularly, is a value-oriented activity is, I would argue, shown by Habermas, Žižek and Deleuze in the way they *critically evaluate values*, by which I mean the way they insist on the cultivation of certain values as against others. In Habermas, for example, this involves insisting on the values of social reciprocity and individual-moral autonomy as against 'consumerism', 'technocratic consciousness' or the ideological 'prejudices' of tradition. In Žižek, this necessitates, among other things, seeing the value in a Kantian notion of ethical responsibility as against the perverse and instrumentalizing ideology of 'totalitarianism'. In Deleuze, for instance, this amounts to emphasizing the ethical significance or value of a liberating and joyous desire as against that which turns desire into an ideological desire for repression. What we can begin to see here is a kind of formal homology at play where the differing, contested, even antagonistic, conceptions of the moral or ethical are nonetheless grounded in accordance with a shared and intuitive concern to critically evaluate values.

Understood in this way, Habermas's, Deleuze's and Žižek's ethical or moral critique of ideology takes on a rather distinctive sense. Yet again, it is important to focus our attention on this as a formalist concern or intuitive gesture, and to understand it more broadly as part and parcel of that which conditions or animates the critique of ideology itself. For just as the practice or activity of engaging in a critique of ideology inevitably presupposes an intuitive call to the real, so too does it necessarily imply an evaluation of values. It is by way of such an evaluation of values that a critique of ideology proceeds, and such a critique cannot proceed without implicitly or intuitively constituting itself as an evaluation of values. Needless to say, this intuitive belief that ideology critique is always-already morally or ethically conditioned is hardly an article of faith among many students or theorists of ideology, and it is indeed quite rare for a theorization of ideology to be couched in explicitly moral or ethical terms.[30] This reflects an understandable apprehension among ideology theorists concerning what is a rather fine line between ethical or moral commitment and reductive and pious moralizing, which then can lead to the worst kind of unreflective ideologizing. Ernesto Laclau, as we saw in chapter 1, would immediately censor and caution us to remain critically sensitive to the 'hegemonic' and, ultimately, ideological consequences that, in his view, necessarily follow from theorizations of the moral and the ethical.[31] And yet, and by implication against theorists such as Laclau, I think it necessary to point out or to make the formalistic argument that there is no escaping the moral or the ethical when it comes to matters of critique, at least if we understand the former as implying an evaluation of values. For instance, Laclau's and Chantal Mouffe's own cool and sober critical analysis of the contingent operation of 'hegemonic' logics in their influential work *Hegemony and Socialist Strategy* tellingly concludes with an essentially ethical affirmation of, what they call, 'radical democracy': a 'form of politics' which is thought to be a necessary corrective to 'dogmatic postulation'.[32] How, to put the question pointedly, can Laclau and Mouffe explain this commitment to 'radical democracy'? Does this commitment to 'radical democracy' not immediately imply an evaluation of values and necessarily reveal itself to be a value-oriented gesture?[33]

What I have been concerned to argue for in this final part of the chapter, and indeed this final part of the book, is a 'critical conception of ideology' that pivots around two intuitions that can be formally extrapolated from Habermas, Deleuze and Žižek – namely, that a critique of ideology intuitively relies on a non-ideological or pre-ideological real, and that it necessarily proceeds on moral or ethical grounds by way of an evaluation of values. It is worth emphasizing or re-emphasizing that the value and significance of the critical ideology theory to be found in Habermas, Deleuze and Žižek extends, in an important sense, beyond the particular ways in which they each express or articulate these intuitions. In other words, it is crucial to develop a critical appreciation of how these intuitions need to be formally understood as part of that which conditions ideology critique in the first instance. Assuming that this formalistic argument is well made or sustainable (a contestable assumption I am well prepared to concede, but well prepared to advocate as you can see from the above), one pressing problem or issue still remains: that is, whether it really matters to theorize formally the intuitions at play in the constitution of ideology critique, or, more dramatically, whether it really matters to think about the status and scope of ideology critique at all. Underpinning these concerns is an understandable impatience with regard to how a seemingly rarefied academic discourse about ideology critique relates to the everyday, how it connects with our experiences in the social. I would like to conclude the book with a couple of brief, but hopefully suggestive, remarks on the subject.

First, and most obviously perhaps, the importance of thinking about the practice of ideology critique is inevitably guided by the sociological recognition that it is part and parcel of actual political discourse, and that it plays a role in the self-understandings and projections of political actors. To take an obvious example, professional politicians, of whatever stripe, are past-masters when it comes to the practice of engaging in ideology critique. Quick to denounce their opponents as 'dogmatic ideologues', and always keen to congratulate themselves on their pragmatism and their ability to adequately read 'the reality of the situation', professional political actors are clearly practitioners of ideology critique, and their actions need to be analysed as such.[34]

Second, beyond the particular and rather confined discourse of professional politics, ideology finds further and broader social expression in, for instance, cultural and media forms. In this context, thinking about ideology and its critique can be immediately tied into existing social formations: that is, the concrete ways in which culture or media forms reproduce and/or contest ideology. In chapter 2, for example, we saw how Habermas showed consumerism to be inextricably related to mass media forms (particularly the rise of a consumer-oriented press) which ideologically frustrate the possibility of developing a democratic public sphere. In chapter 7, I used Deleuze's Spinozian notion of an ethics beyond ideology to critically analyse certain modes of subjectivity at play in Paul Thomas Anderson's *Magnolia*. And, to take but one other example, we saw in chapters 4 and 5 how Žižek theorized a kind of freedom or autonomy from the social-ideological field by way of an analysis of the actions of Keyser Soeze in Brian Singer's *The Usual Suspects*. What is expressed here, I would argue, is a much-needed form of cultural or media literacy with regard to the concrete operations of ideology and its critique in the social. Of course, cultural or media literacy such as this can help us to critically come to terms with the forms of ideology we concretely encounter in social life if, and only if, we have a degree of clarity in our minds about the stakes of the activity of critique itself. The importance of Habermas, Deleuze and Žižek, as I have stressed, is that they explicitly help in this respect. That is to say, they help us by animating or giving meaning to the idea that the critique of ideology intuitively implies the reliance on a non-ideological or pre-ideological real, and that it intuitively necessitates a moral or ethical evaluation of values.

Notes

1 Introducing the Critical Conception of Ideology

1. On this point, see John Thompson, *Ideology and Modern Culture: Critical Social Theory in the Era of Mass Communication* (Cambridge, 1990), p. 30.
2. On this point, and for a more general appreciation of the importance of de Tracy's ideology theory, see I. Mackenzie and S. Malesevic, 'Introduction: de Tracy's legacy', in S. Malesevic and I. Mackenzie (eds), *Ideology After Poststructuralism* (London, 2002), pp. 1–8.
3. On this point, see Howard Williams, *Concepts of Ideology* (Sussex, 1988), p. xi.
4. Ibid., p. xi.
5. Karl Marx and Friedrich Engels, *The German Ideology* (London, 1974), p. 47.
6. Ibid., p. 64.
7. 'Modern scholarship', as Michael Freeden puts it, 'still labours heavily under the mid-nineteenth-century shadow of Marx and Engels.' Michael Freeden, *Ideologies and Political Theory: A Conceptual Approach* (Oxford, 1996), p. 14.
8. Paul Ricoeur, *Hermeneutics and the Human Sciences* (Cambridge, 1981), p. 227.
9. Ibid., p. 235.
10. Ibid., p. 243.
11. Freeden, *Ideologies and Political Theory*, p. 77.
12. Interestingly, this interpretation resonates strongly with Žižek's reading of the film. See, for example, Slavoj Žižek, *Organs Without Bodies: Deleuze and Consequences* (London, 2004), pp. 173–4.
13. For this kind of reading of *Fight Club*, see A. Taubin, 'So good it hurts', *Sight and Sound*, 9, 11 (1999), 16–18. Also see J. Craine and S. C. Aitken, 'Street fighting: placing the crisis of masculinity in David Fincher's *Fight Club*', *GeoJournal*, 59, 4 (2004), 289–96.
14. 'Ultimately, ideologies are configurations of decontested meanings of political concepts'. Freeden, *Ideologies and Political Theory*, p. 76.
15. Ibid., p. 55.
16. Ibid., p. 59.
17. Ibid., p. 57.
18. See, for example, F. Jameson, 'Postmodernism and the market', in Slavoj Žižek (ed.), *Mapping Ideology* (London, 1994), p. 279. Or, R. Rorty, 'Feminism, ideology and deconstruction: a pragmatist view', in Žižek (ed.), *Mapping Ideology*, p. 229.

[19] Ricoeur, *Hermeneutics and the Human Sciences*, p. 230.
[20] Freeden, *Ideologies and Political Theory*, p. 15.
[21] See the concluding part of chapter 8.
[22] See, for example, the third and concluding part of chapter 2 and the first part of chapter 3.
[23] See, most specifically, the third and concluding part of chapter 4. And, also see the first part of chapter 5.
[24] See the third and concluding part of chapter 6.
[25] See the final part of chapter 6, and, more particularly, the first part of chapter 7.
[26] The key here will be to argue for this intuition in a particularly formal way or on a formalistic basis. See the final part of chapter 8.
[27] Of course, it is far from unproblematic to use the terms 'ethical' and 'moral' interchangeably as the precise status, and the relative importance, given to these terms has been the subject of so much debate in recent social and political theory. The crucial point for me in the present work is to insist on the broad or formal intuition that Habermas, Žižek and Deleuze all provide us with a critique of ideology that proceeds on certain moral or ethical grounds, however the 'moral' or 'ethical' is construed in each case. The importance or significance of this broad intuition will inevitably become the focus of my considered attention in the final part of chapter 8.
[28] See the second and third parts of chapter 3.
[29] See the first part of chapter 5.
[30] See the concluding part of chapter 7.
[31] B. Susser, 'The domains of ideological discourse', *The Journal of Political Ideologies*, 1, 2 (1996), 165–81.
[32] See Freeden, *Ideologies and Political Theory*, p. 28.
[33] Charles Taylor, *Multiculturalism and the Politics of Recognition* (New Jersey, 1992), pp. 72–3.
[34] Ibid., p. 73.
[35] Ibid., p. 25.
[36] See Freeden, *Ideologies and Political Theory*, p. 515.
[37] See E. Laclau, 'Deconstruction, pragmatism, hegemony', in C. Mouffe (ed.), *Deconstruction and Pragmatism* (London, 1996), p. 53.
[38] See the final part of chapter 8.
[39] You will notice that in the introductory chapters to each thinker (i.e., chapter 2 on Habermas, chapter 4 on Žižek and chapter 6 on Deleuze) I do quite a bit of groundwork before explicitly engaging with their particular theories of ideology, and that I thematically pivot these discussions around the issues or concepts of 'rationality' and 'subjectivity'. In a sense, of course, this discursive tactic or strategy is quite arbitrary, but it will nonetheless prove useful in providing some initial thematic structure and focus, which will, in turn, help us come to terms with certain key concepts

in their, inevitably different and idiosyncratic, theories of ideology. For example, we shall see that Habermas's ideas about rationality and subjectivity will introduce us to the key concepts of the 'communicative' and the 'postmetaphysical'. More specifically, we will witness how Habermas's communicative or postmetaphysical conceptions of reason and the self imply, or relate to, a broader notion of the 'real', a 'real' that is 'non-ideological' or 'pre-ideological'. We shall see that Žižek's musings on rationality and subjectivity will introduce us to a whole series of psychoanalytically inflected concepts – i.e., 'fantasy', 'subjective destitution', 'the Real', 'antagonism', 'the symbolic' – that are central to his understanding of the status and function of ideology in social life. We shall see that Deleuze's critique of reason and his advocacy of, what we will call, a 'vitalist' conception of subjectivity will introduce us to the crucial notion of 'desire', and, in turn, to the critique of ideology implied by his (and Guattari's) theory of desire.

40 Consider, for instance, Žižek's suggestion that David Lynch's *Lost Highway* profoundly shows how 'social reality' is structured in accordance with a 'fantasy' that is constitutively antagonistic or, as he says, necessarily 'decomposed'. See Slavoj Žižek, *The Art of the Ridiculous Sublime* (Seattle, 2000), p. 13. Or, think about how Deleuze insists that Orson Welles's *It's All True* forces us to reckon with what he calls 'the powers of the false', where this implies an ethics and a politics anchored in the constitutive forces of the 'body'. See Gilles Deleuze, *Cinema 2: The Time-Image* (London, 1989), p. 239.

41 This is a point that I will take up and develop in parts two and three of chapter 7.

2 Habermas's Ideology Theory

1 See, for example, Shane O'Neill, *Impartiality in Context: Grounding Justice in a Pluralist World* (New York, 1997).
2 See Peter Dews, (ed.), *Habermas: A Critical Reader* (Oxford, 1999). For a sociological and media studies perspective on Habermas's critical and ideology theory, see: William Outhwaite, *Habermas: A Critical Introduction* (Cambridge, 1994); N. Garnham, 'The media and the public sphere', in C. Calhoun (ed.), *Habermas and the Public Sphere* (London, 1992), pp. 359–76.
3 Jürgen Habermas, *Postmetaphysical Thinking* (Cambridge, 1998), pp. 115–48.
4 Ibid., p. 135.
5 Ibid., p. 118.
6 This is the image that is painted of the 'philosopher-ruler'. See Plato, *The Republic* (London, 1975), p. 293.

7 Habermas, *Postmetaphysical Thinking*, p. 31.
8 Immanuel Kant, *Groundwork of the Metaphysic of Morals* (New York, 1964), p. 101. On the Kantian 'kingdom of ends', see Howard Williams, *Kant's Political Philosophy* (Oxford, 1983), p. 261.
9 Habermas, *Postmetaphysical Thinking*, p. 117.
10 Ibid., p. 29.
11 Ibid., p. 117.
12 Ibid., p. 130.
13 See, for example, Richard Rorty, *Contingency, Irony and Solidarity* (Cambridge, 1989).
14 Habermas, *Postmetaphysical Thinking*, p. 131.
15 Ibid., p. 139.
16 Ibid., p. 139.
17 Jürgen Habermas, *Communication and the Evolution of Society* (London, 1979), p. 2.
18 Jürgen Habermas, 'Richard Rorty's pragmatic turn', in R. Brandom (ed.), *Rorty and his Critics* (Oxford, 2000), p. 46.
19 Habermas, *Postmetaphysical Thinking*, p. 142.
20 Habermas, 'Richard Rorty's pragmatic turn', p. 46.
21 Ibid., p. 48. For further discussion of the interplay between the 'context-dependent' and 'context-transcendent' aspects of Habermas's theory of communicative action, see R. Porter and K. A. Porter, 'Habermas and the pragmatics of communication: a Deleuze-Guattarian critique', *Social Semiotics*, 13, 2 (2003), 134–7.
22 We shall see that Žižek is closer to Habermas on this issue than Deleuze. While Žižek is certainly more ambivalent than Habermas about the concept of reason, he nonetheless is content to argue for its progressive use in ideology critique. I will introduce and discuss Žižek's particular notion of reason or rationality in chapter 4. Deleuze, on the other hand, is clearly more hostile to the notion, and is more concerned, after a certain Nietzschean fashion, to question its utility in matters of critique. This is a point that I will develop in chapter 6. Of course, Habermas would be critical of Deleuze's anti-rationalism, seeing the latter's critique and rejection of reason as inherently contradictory or as necessarily lapsing into, what he would call, a 'performative contradiction'. I will explicitly consider this Habermasian critique of Deleuze in chapter 8.
23 Habermas, *Postmetaphysical Thinking*, p. 153.
24 Ibid., p. 154.
25 Ibid., p. 158.
26 Ibid., p. 170.
27 Ibid., p. 170.
28 Ibid., p. 184.
29 Ibid., p. 185–6.

30 Ibid., p. 186.
31 Ibid., p. 184. This image of the subject (whether individual or collective) exercising autonomy and standing against the conventional or traditional morality of the community is one that I will again take up toward the end of chapter 3. Or, more particularly, I will explore Habermas's notion of 'moral autonomy', using the film *Pleasantville* as a cinematic backcloth to tease out some of the implications of this important notion.
32 Habermas, *Postmetaphysical Thinking*, p. 185.
33 For a clear declarative statement on the 'communicative' nature of the 'real', see Jürgen Habermas, *The Past as Future* (Cambridge, 1994), p. 102. As stated, I will revisit and develop this crucial notion in the first part of chapter 3.
34 Habermas, *Postmetaphysical Thinking*, p. 103.
35 Ibid., p. 103.
36 Habermas, *The Past as Future*, p. 102.
37 Habermas, 'Richard Rorty's pragmatic turn', p. 46.
38 Ibid., p. 46.
39 I will focus explicitly on these issues in chapter 8. That is to say, in the first part of chapter 8 I shall mount certain Žižekian arguments against Habermas's 'transcendentalism' and 'normativism' before turning, in the second part of the chapter, to a Deleuzian critique of the same.
40 Jürgen Habermas, *The Structural Transformation of the Public Sphere* (Cambridge, 1992), p. 181.
41 Ibid., p. 161.
42 Ibid., p. 171.
43 Ibid., p. 161.
44 Ibid., p. 172.
45 I will further develop this point in the next chapter. Or, more specifically, we will see how 'strategic action' or, what Habermas also calls, the 'instrumental use of language' can be regarded as an 'ideological' truncation or repression of the normative and communicative structure of social relations. See the first part of chapter 3. Also see the subsequent parts of the chapter where I broaden the discussion by considering Habermas's (normatively oriented) ideology critique of 'technology', 'scientism' and the 'prejudices' of 'tradition'.

3 Habermas's Moral Critique of Ideology

1 Jürgen Habermas, *The Theory of Communicative Action Vol. 1: Reason and the Rationalization of Society* (London, 1984), p. 288.
2 Ibid., p. 289.
3 Ibid., p. 289.

4 Ibid., p. 289.
5 Ibid., p. 289.
6 Ibid., p. 289.
7 For a more detailed overview, and critique, of Habermas's use of Austin in arguing for the priority of communicative action, see William Outhwaite, *Habermas: A Critical Introduction* (Cambridge, 1994), p. 46.
8 Habermas, *The Theory of Communicative Action Vol. 1*, p. 305.
9 The crucial distinction that Habermas draws between 'communicative action' and 'strategic action', and the priority or significance he invests in the former over the latter, can be, and has been, subject to much critical interrogation. In the concluding chapter, I will draw on Deleuze directly to question this distinction and, in so doing, emphasize the problematic status of Habermas's 'normativism'. See part two of chapter 8.
10 Habermas, *The Theory of Communicative Action Vol. 1*, p. 306.
11 Jürgen Habermas, *Postmetaphysical Thinking* (Cambridge, 1998), p. 186.
12 Jürgen Habermas, *The Past as Future* (Cambridge, 1994), p. 102.
13 For a critical analysis of this point, see R. Porter and K. A. Porter, 'Habermas and the pragmatics of communication: a Deleuze-Guattarian critique', *Social Semiotics*, 13, 2 (2003), 129–45.
14 Habermas, *Postmetaphysical Thinking*, p. 84.
15 For a detailed and impressive discussion of Habermas's critique of positivism, see Thomas McCarthy, *The Critical Theory of Jürgen Habermas* (Cambridge, 1984), pp. 40–52.
16 See Thomas Hobbes, *Leviathan* (London, 1968).
17 On this point, see McCarthy, *The Critical Theory of Jürgen Habermas*, p. 1.
18 Jürgen Habermas, *The Habermas Reader* (Cambridge, 1996), pp. 64–5.
19 Jürgen Habermas, *The Structural Transformation of the Public Sphere* (Cambridge, 1992), p. 181.
20 Jürgen Habermas, *The Future of Human Nature* (Cambridge, 2003).
21 Ibid., pp. 11–12.
22 Ibid., p. 13.
23 Ibid., p. 14.
24 Ibid., p. 11.
25 Ibid., p. 6.
26 On Habermas's profound debt to Kant, see, for example, Jürgen Habermas, *Moral Consciousness and Communicative Action* (Cambridge, 1990), pp. 195–215.
27 Habermas, *The Future of Human Nature*, p. 11. This, clearly, is not to imply that such a 'formalist' approach is beyond critical scrutiny. Indeed, one of the most constant criticisms raised against Habermas's moral theory is that it implies a kind of 'formalism' or 'abstract universalism' which is particularly insensitive to the specific contexts, or forms of 'ethical life', in which moral problems arise. For his response to this critique,

see Habermas, *Moral Consciousness and Communicative Action*, pp. 195–215.
28 Habermas, *The Future of Human Nature*, p. 10. Or, Habermas, *Moral Consciousness and Communicative Action*, p. 162.
29 Cinematically, or visually, this unquenchable or irrepressible desire for freedom is represented through the transformation of figures from black and white into full colour. Importantly, each and every one of the principal characters in the film undergoes this seemingly inevitable and irreversible change. We will look at specific characters below.
30 For an appreciation of this point, see J. Hoberman, 'Under the rainbow', *Sight and Sound*, 9, 1 (1999), 14–16.
31 Of course, and as we have already seen, Habermas theorizes the autonomy of the subject in communicative terms. That is to say, autonomy or freedom is thought to be irrepressibly and crucially part of the sense of self formed through communicative action. On this point, see the first part of this chapter. And, for a fuller discussion of Habermas's theory of subjectivity, see the second part of chapter 2.
32 Quoted in McCarthy, *The Critical Theory of Jürgen Habermas*, p. 183.
33 Of course, some critics would suggest that the ideological 'prejudices' of tradition can never really be critically surmounted as such. As we saw in chapter 1, Paul Ricoeur would argue that our 'knowledge' about the social, and our sense of self, is always-already ideologically predicated on a kind of 'social belonging' which is pre-reflexively or unreflectively tied to 'one or several traditions'. See Paul Ricoeur, *Hermeneutics and the Human Sciences* (Cambridge, 1981), p. 243. I will come back to Ricoeur in the final part of chapter 8.
34 Habermas, *Moral Consciousness and Communicative Action*, p. 162.
35 For a discussion of Habermas's critique of ideology as 'systematically distorted communication', see, for example, Outhwaite, *Habermas: A Critical Introduction*, p. 34.
36 We see this most explicitly in Mr Johnson's desire to capture the beauty of Betty through painting her.

4 Žižek's Ideology Theory

1 As will become clear during the course of this and the next chapter, Lacan is a dominant, ever-present and fundamental influence on Žižek's thought. On the centrality of the Lacanian concept of 'the Real' in Žižek's thought, see Sarah Kay, *Žižek: A Critical Introduction* (Cambridge, 2003), pp. 1–16.
2 Slavoj Žižek, *The Plague of Fantasies* (London, 1997).
3 Ibid., p. 1.

NOTES 145

4 Ibid., p. 7.
5 Ibid., p. 9.
6 Ibid., p. 9.
7 Ibid., p. 9.
8 Ibid., p. 10. Reference to the concept of 'antagonism' occurs constantly throughout Žižek's writings. I will come back to this important notion at various points in this and the next chapter.
9 Slavoj Žižek, *The Sublime Object of Ideology* (London, 1989), p. 126.
10 Ibid., p. 125–6.
11 Žižek, *The Plague of Fantasies*, p. 16.
12 See Paul Auster, *The New York Trilogy* (London, 1987). For example, in 'City of Glass' we find Daniel Quinn, the central character of the story, reflecting and fantasizing about the precise moment of his conception (supposedly his parents' wedding night), and secretly celebrating his birthday on their wedding anniversary.
13 Žižek, *The Plague of Fantasies*, p. 16.
14 There is, as Žižek would say, a certain 'madness' implied by the use of reason. See, for example, Slavoj Žižek, *The Ticklish Subject* (London, 1999), p. 35. I will come back to this point in the third and final part of this chapter.
15 See Žižek, *The Ticklish Subject*, p. 347.
16 Ibid., p. 175.
17 For an accessible and useful introduction to Žižek's theory of subjectivity – and to the broad themes of Žižekian thought more generally – see Kay, *Žižek: A Critical Introduction*, pp. 82–90. For a more particular consideration of how Žižek theorizes the subject's experience of ideology, see R. Porter, 'A world beyond ideology?: strains in Slavoj Žižek's ideology critique', in S. Malesevic and I. Mackenzie (eds), *Ideology After Poststructuralism* (London, 2002), pp. 43–63.
18 Žižek, *The Ticklish Subject*, p. 171–244.
19 L. Althusser, 'Ideology and ideological state apparatuses', in S. Žižek (ed.), *Mapping Ideology* (London, 1994), p. 131.
20 Ibid., p. 111.
21 Žižek, *The Ticklish Subject*, p. 232.
22 Ibid., p. 232. The suggestion that Althusser fails to adequately theorize the possibility of challenging the hegemony of the state is perhaps the most repeated criticism levelled at his theory of ideology. For a possible reappraisal and response to this critique, see C. Williams, 'Ideology and imaginary: returning to Althusser', in S. Malesevic and I. Mackenzie (eds), *Ideology After Poststructuralism* (London, 2002), pp. 28–42.
23 Žižek, *The Ticklish Subject*, p. 130.
24 Ibid., p. 135.
25 Ibid., pp. 187–8.
26 Ibid., p. 188.

[27] Ibid., p. 235.
[28] Ibid., pp. 237–8.
[29] Ibid., p. 232.
[30] Žižek, *The Sublime Object of Ideology*, pp. 230–31.
[31] Slavoj Žižek, *The Fragile Absolute* (London, 2000), pp. 149–50.
[32] Žižek, *The Sublime Object of Ideology*, p. 230.
[33] For a useful and accessible discussion of Žižek's concept of the 'big Other', see Kay, *Žižek: A Critical Introduction*, p. 159.
[34] The question that can be raised here concerns whether there is a kind of normatively irresponsible and dangerous heroism in Žižek, where the autonomy of the subject is judged only in terms of its wilful and singular resolve, a resolve that may turn out to be devoid of all moral content. I will address this point explicitly in the eighth and concluding chapter.
[35] Žižek, *The Fragile Absolute*, p. 150.
[36] On the negativity or, what he also calls, 'radical negativity' of 'the Real', see Žižek, *The Sublime Object of Ideology*, pp. 205–6.
[37] See Žižek, *The Sublime Object of Ideology*, p. 87.
[38] Žižek, *The Plague of Fantasies*, p. 217.
[39] Žižek, *The Sublime Object of Ideology*, p. 164.
[40] Ibid., p. 99.
[41] Žižek, *The Ticklish Subject*, p. 35.
[42] Ibid., p. 35.
[43] See, for example, Žižek, *The Plague of Fantasies*, p. 7.
[44] Žižek, *The Ticklish Subject*, pp. 237–8. This is not to say that Žižek would simply dismiss 'hysterical provocation' as always inherently conservative. Indeed, we shall see in the next chapter how the 'hysterical subject' can mount a critique against authority and ideological orthodoxy. On the ethico-political importance of 'hysteria' to Žižek's critical theory, see Kay, *Žižek: A Critical Introduction*, pp. 164–5.
[45] On the 'madness' implied in and through the use of reason, see, for example, Žižek, *The Ticklish Subject*, p. 35.
[46] Žižek, *The Sublime Object of Ideology*, p. 33.
[47] Ibid., p. 49.
[48] A good contemporary example of this, for Žižek, is the hold that 'cynicism', or what he also calls 'cynical reason', has over our particular sense of what constitutes the 'reality' of the social. That is to say, the subject of 'late capitalism' tends, Žižek argues, to set itself at a 'cynical distance' from the 'social', and this distancing movement precipitates a certain blindness to 'the structuring power of ideological fantasy'. I will develop this point and give it a fuller and more concrete sense in the final part of the next chapter.
[49] This is a point that I also take up in Porter, 'A world beyond ideology?', p. 54.
[50] Žižek (ed.), *Mapping Ideology*, p. 17.

5 Žižek's Ethical Critique of Ideology

1. On the relationship between 'freedom' and 'the Real', see Slavoj Žižek, *The Abyss of Freedom* (Michigan, 1997), pp. 31–2. Also, see Slavoj Žižek, *The Indivisible Remainder: An Essay on Schelling and Related Matters* (London, 1996), pp. 33–4.
2. See, for example, S. Žižek, 'Beyond discourse analysis', in E. Laclau, *New Reflections on the Revolution of Our Time* (London, 1990), p. 259.
3. Slavoj Žižek, *The Plague of Fantasies* (London, 1997), p. 214.
4. Slavoj Žižek, *The Sublime Object of Ideology* (London, 1989), pp. 172–3.
5. For further discussion and analysis of this point, see R. Porter, 'A world beyond ideology?: strains in Slavoj Žižek's ideology critique', in S. Malesevic and I. Mackenzie (eds), *Ideology After Poststructuralism* (London, 2002), pp. 55–6.
6. Slavoj Žižek, *Did Some Say Totalitarianism?: Five Interventions in the (Mis)use of a Notion* (London, 2001), p. 3.
7. Ibid., p. 243.
8. Ibid., p. 243.
9. Ibid., pp. 243–4.
10. Ibid., p. 242.
11. Slavoj Žižek, *The Ticklish Subject*, (London, 1999), p. 199.
12. Slavoj Žižek (ed.), *Mapping Ideology* (London, 1994), p. 1.
13. Žižek, *The Plague of Fantasies*, p. 221.
14. More generally, it is well worth acknowledging that Žižek's particular reading of Kant is quite idiosyncratic, that he is less systematic, compared with Habermas for example, in his treatment of Kantian concepts. As has been pointed out to me by Howard Williams, Žižek's engagement with Kant is one that stresses the 'aesthetic' side of his work. We see this quite clearly in Žižek's discussion of the Kantian concept of the 'Sublime', and in his creative use of this concept in advancing his theory of ideology. See, most obviously, Žižek, *The Sublime Object of Ideology*, p. 201. In this regard, Žižek's work or critical theory resonates with the 'postmodernism' of Lyotard, particularly as the latter is also clearly concerned to critically put to use, or to creatively reconstruct, the Kantian 'Sublime'. See, for example, Jean-Francois Lyotard, *The Postmodern Condition: A Report on Knowledge* (Manchester, 1994), pp. 77–9.
15. Žižek, *The Plague of Fantasies*, p. 231.
16. Ibid., p. 231.
17. On the resistance of the 'hysterical' subject to 'interpellation', see Slavoj Žižek, *For They Know Not What They Do: Enjoyment as a Political Factor* (London, 1991), p. 101.
18. 'Stepping out of (what we experience as) ideology', Žižek paradoxically asserts, 'is the very form of our enslavement to it'. Žižek, *Mapping Ideology*, p. 6. I will again come back to this point in the first part of chapter 8.

[19] Žižek, *The Plague of Fantasies*, p. 222.
[20] I also deal with this issue in R. Porter, 'The singularity of the political', in A. Finlayson and J. Valentine (eds), *Politics and Post-structuralism* (Edinburgh, 2002), p. 204.
[21] Žižek, *The Plague of Fantasies*, p. 223.
[22] Ibid., pp. 229–30.
[23] Žižek, *The Sublime Object of Ideology*, p. 33.
[24] Ibid., pp. 31–3.
[25] For an appreciation of the influence, significance and implications of Beck's notion of a 'risk society', see Barbara Adam, Ulrich Beck and Joost Van Loon (eds), *The Risk Society and Beyond* (London, 2000).
[26] Slavoj Žižek, *On Belief* (London, 2001), p. 116.
[27] On the 'objectivity' of ideological belief, see Žižek, *The Sublime Object of Ideology*, pp. 34–6.
[28] On this point, see M. Moriarty, 'Žižek, religion and ideology', *Paragraph*, 24 (2001), 125–39.
[29] Žižek, *The Ticklish Subject*, p. 135.
[30] Žižek, *On Belief*, p. 148.
[31] In particular, we shall see that the 'heroism' implied by Žižek's ethics, or the supposedly 'heroic' terms on which his notion of the ethical subject is justified, is directly criticizable from Habermas's point of view. This is a point I will make in the concluding chapter.
[32] Žižek, *On Belief*, p. 148.
[33] Ibid., pp. 148–51.
[34] Ibid., p. 148.
[35] See, for example, Žižek, *The Sublime Object of Ideology*, p. 28.

6 Deleuze's Ideology Theory

[1] This, of course, is not to say that Habermas fails to appreciate the problematic nature of reason, or that the use of reason in the social world can be subject to ideological constraints. See, most obviously, Jürgen Habermas, *The Theory of Communicative Action Vol. 1: Reason and the Rationalization of Society* (London, 1984).
[2] Gilles Deleuze, *Nietzsche and Philosophy* (London, 1986), p. 91.
[3] Ibid., p. 91.
[4] I. Kant, 'What is enlightenment?', in S. Lotringer and L. Hochroth (eds), *The Politics of Truth: Michel Foucault* (New York, 1995), p. 7.
[5] Ibid., pp. 7–8.
[6] For a good discussion of this point, see Iain Mackenzie, *The Idea of Pure Critique* (London, 2004), pp. 9–20.
[7] Deleuze, *Nietzsche and Philosophy*, p. 91.

[8] For a more detailed critical evaluation of Deleuze's critique of Kantian reason, see Mackenzie, *The Idea of Pure Critique*, pp. 11–20.
[9] Gilles Deleuze and Félix Guattari, *Anti-Oedipus: Capitalism and Schizophrenia* (London, 1984).
[10] Ibid., p. 1.
[11] On the 'superhuman eye' of the camera, see Gilles Deleuze, *Cinema 1: The Movement-Image* (London, 1992), p. 40.
[12] Or, more generally put, desire functions, for Deleuze and Guattari, to produce the 'reality' of the 'social field'. I will come back to this important point in the final part of the chapter. For a broader discussion of this issue, and for an appreciation of how this conception of 'desire' implies a critique of psychoanalysis, see Phillip Goodchild, *Deleuze and Guattari: An Introduction to the Politics of Desire* (London, 1996), pp. 125–6.
[13] Deleuze and Guattari, *Anti-Oedipus*, p. 28.
[14] Ibid., p. 28.
[15] 'Everything I have written is vitalistic, at least I hope it is.' Gilles Deleuze, *Negotiations* (New York, 1995), p. 143.
[16] Gilles Deleuze, *Foucault* (Minneapolis, 1988), p. 106.
[17] For further discussion of this point or issue, see Keith Ansell Pearson, *Germinal Life: The Difference and Repetition of Deleuze* (London, 1999), pp. 214–24.
[18] For a comprehensive survey and discussion of Deleuze's theory of subjectivity, see C. V. Boundas, 'Serialization and subject-formation', in C. V. Boundas and D. Olkowski (eds), *Gilles Deleuze and the Theater of Philosophy* (New York, 1994), pp. 99–116.
[19] Gilles Deleuze, *Empiricism and Subjectivity: An Essay on Hume's Theory of Human Nature* (New York, 1991), p. 85.
[20] Ibid., p. 85.
[21] Ibid., p. 101.
[22] Deleuze, *Cinema 1: The Movement-Image*, p. 200.
[23] Ibid., p. 200.
[24] Ibid., p. x.
[25] Deleuze warns against the stupidity and maliciousness of 'cartoon' versions of the Nietzschean 'superman' in his work on Foucault. See Deleuze, *Foucault*, p. 130.
[26] For a Deleuzian critique of the will 'that wants power', see Deleuze, *Nietzsche and Philosophy*, p. 85.
[27] On the importance of an essentially impersonal or depersonalizing 'outside' to the constitution and reconstruction of subjectivity, see Deleuze, *Foucault*, pp. 95–6.
[28] Although it is important to point out that Foucault does not, as is often suggested, totally dismiss the concept of ideology out of hand; rather, he expresses his reservations by merely stating that he finds the notion

'difficult', warning against using it 'without circumspection'. On this point see D. Coole, 'The dialectics of the real', in S. Malesevic and I. Mackenzie (eds), *Ideology After Poststructuralism* (London, 2002), pp. 119–20.
29. Gilles Deleuze and Félix Guattari, *A Thousand Plateaus: Capitalism and Schizophrenia* (London, 1988), p. 4.
30. See, for example, Claire Colebrook, *Gilles Deleuze* (London, 2002), p. 92.
31. On this point, see Brian Massumi, *A User's Guide to Capitalism and Schizophrenia: Deviations from Deleuze and Guattari* (London, 1993), p. 105.
32. Deleuze and Guattari, *Anti-Oedipus*, p. 24.
33. Ibid., p. 101.
34. 'The first principle of philosophy is that Universals explain nothing but must themselves be explained.' Gilles Deleuze and Félix Guattari, *What is Philosophy?* (London, 1994), p. 7. Also see Gilles Deleuze and Claire Parnet, *Dialogues* (London, 1987), p. x. For a good discussion of the critical-political implications of Deleuze and Guattari's 'constructivism', see I. Mackenzie, 'Creativity as criticism: the philosophical constructivism of Deleuze and Guattari', *Radical Philosophy*, 86 (1997), 7–18.
35. The 'fundamental problem of political philosophy is still precisely the one that Spinoza saw so clearly . . . "Why do men fight *for* their servitude . . . as though it were their salvation?" How can people possibly reach the point of shouting: "More taxes! Less bread!?" ' Deleuze and Guattari, *Anti-Oedipus*, p. 29.
36. Ibid., pp. 28–9.
37. This is not to say that the Deleuzian distinction between the real and the ideological is unproblematic or beyond critical reproach. Indeed, we shall see in the eighth and concluding chapter how this very distinction can be problematized or subject to critical interrogation from both a Habermasian and Žižekian perspective.

7 Deleuze's Ethical Critique of Ideology

1. On this point, see M. Hardt, 'The withering of civil society', in E. Kaufman and K. J. Heller (eds), *Deleuze and Guattari*, (Minneapolis, 1998), p. 23.
2. Gilles Deleuze, *Negotiations* (New York, 1995), p. 182.
3. Ibid., pp. 177–9.
4. Ibid., p. 182.
5. On the decisive political influence or controlling tendencies of contemporary capitalism, see Gilles Deleuze and Félix Guattari, *What is Philosophy?* (London, 1994), p. 106. Also, see Slavoj Žižek (ed.), *Mapping Ideology* (London, 1994), p. 1.
6. Deleuze, *Negotiations*, p. 181.

7. For an accessible and useful survey of some of the implications that follow from Deleuze's ethical theory, see D. Smith, 'The place of ethics in Deleuze's philosophy', in Kaufman and Heller (eds), *Deleuze and Guattari*, pp. 251–69. Also, see Michael Hardt, *Gilles Deleuze: An Apprenticeship in Philosophy* (London, 1993), pp. 26–55.
8. Gilles Deleuze, *Cinema 2: The Time-Image* (London, 1989); G. Deleuze, 'Having an idea in cinema', in Kaufman and Heller (eds), *Deleuze and Guattari*, pp. 14–19.
9. Deleuze, 'Having an idea in cinema', p. 19.
10. Deleuze, *Cinema 2: The Time-Image*, p. 215.
11. The idea that political cinema is about representing 'the people' is, for Deleuze, an essentially 'classical' rather than 'modern' notion. See Deleuze, *Cinema 2: The Time-Image*, p. 216.
12. This notion of a perceptually subjective point-of-view shot is taken from David Bordwell and Kristin Thompson, *Film Art: An Introduction* (New York, 2004), p. 85.
13. For a discussion of the 'fetishistic spilt' in the structure of subjectivity, see, for example, Slavoj Žižek, *The Sublime Object of Ideology* (London, 1989), p. 34.
14. On the use of the whip pan, and for an analysis of how a pan can be used as a point-of-view shot, see Bordwell and Thompson, *Film Art: An Introduction*, p. 401 and p. 269.
15. For further discussion of this concept of 'liberty', see Gilles Deleuze, *The Fold: Leibniz and the Baroque* (London, 1993), pp. 70–3.
16. Indeed, this is a point made by Thomas Anderson himself when he refers to the 'Wise Up' scene as 'something very sweet, sentimental in the best way'. See M. Olsen, 'Singing in the rain', *Sight and Sound*, 10, 3 (2000), 27.
17. This scene can also be considered redemptive from Jim's perspective. For we see that just as Donnie's monologue ends (i.e., with the close-up of Jim which confirms his empathy for Donnie), Jim's lost gun – the very thing that has come to signify Jim's regret and belief in his own stupidity – miraculously reappears by literally falling from the sky.
18. Gilles Deleuze, *Spinoza: Practical Philosophy* (San Francisco, 1988); Gilles Deleuze, *Expressionism in Philosophy: Spinoza* (New York, 1992).
19. Deleuze, *Spinoza: Practical Philosophy*, pp. 22–3.
20. For a good discussion of this kind of Deleuzian ethics of joy, where 'ethics of joy' signifies an intersubjective or trans-subjective encounter and an increase in the 'power' of the desiring subject, see Paul Patton, *Deleuze and the Political* (London, 2000), pp. 76–7.
21. Indeed, this kind of reaction – of surprise, of awe in the face of the 'sublime' – is integrated within the narrative structure of the film and reflected in the response of Phil, the nurse. Dumbfounded, and slightly disturbed, he asks himself: 'why are frogs falling from the sky?'

8 Conclusion

1. This notion of a 'performative contradiction' is one extrapolated from Habermas's, now famous, critique of Michel Foucault. See Jürgen Habermas, *The Philosophical Discourse of Modernity* (Cambridge, 1990), pp. 238–93.
2. Slavoj Žižek (ed.), *Mapping Ideology* (London, 1994), p. 17.
3. This is a question that I also raise against Žižek in R. Porter, 'A world beyond ideology?: strains in Slavoj Žižek's ideology critique', in S. Malesevic and I. Mackenzie (eds), *Ideology After Poststructuralism* (London, 2002), p. 49.
4. Žižek (ed.), *Mapping Ideology*, p. 6.
5. See S. Žižek, 'Beyond discourse analysis', in E. Laclau, *New Reflections on the Revolution of Our Time* (London, 1990), p. 259.
6. Jürgen Habermas, *The Past as Future* (Cambridge, 1994), p. 102.
7. Žižek, 'Beyond discourse analysis', p. 259.
8. This critical tension between the philosophical and sociological tendencies in Habermas's thinking is brought into sharp focus by his colleague and long-time friend, Karl Otto Apel. See, for example, K. O. Apel, 'Openly strategic uses of language: a transcendental-pragmatic perspective', in P. Dews (ed.), *Habermas: A Critical Reader* (Oxford, 1999), p. 281.
9. Žižek, 'Beyond discourse analysis', p. 259.
10. The question of the rather problematic status of Habermas's 'transcendentalism' is one that I also deal with in R. Porter, 'Ideology', in I. Mackenzie (ed.), *Political Concepts: A Reader and a Guide* (Edinburgh, 2005), pp. 525–52.
11. Gilles Deleuze and Félix Guattari, *A Thousand Plateaus: Capitalism and Schizophrenia* (London, 1988), p. 76.
12. Ibid., p. 76.
13. Ibid., p. 79.
14. Jürgen Habermas, *Moral Consciousness and Communicative Action* (Cambridge, 1990), p. 102.
15. For further elaboration of this point from a Deleuzian perspective, see R. Porter and K. A. Porter, 'Habermas and the pragmatics of communication: A Deleuze-Guattarian critique', *Social Semiotics*, 13, 2 (2003), 129–45.
16. This point is also taken up against Habermas, albeit in a slightly different way, by Richard Rorty. See, for example, R. Rorty, 'Universality and truth', in R. Brandom (ed.), *Rorty and his Critics* (Oxford, 2000), p. 10.
17. See Habermas, *The Philosophical Discourse of Modernity*, p. 127.
18. Ibid., p. 127.
19. For further discussion of the implications that follow from Habermas's implicit and explicit critique of Deleuze's Nietzscheanism, and for a possible Deleuzian response, see R. Porter, 'Deleuze, geophilosophy, criticism' (unpublished Ph.D. thesis, Queens University, Belfast, 1999), 78–166.

[20] See Slavoj Žižek, *Tarrying with the Negative: Kant, Hegel and the Critique of Ideology*, (Durham, 1993), p. 219.
[21] J. J. Lecercle, 'The pedagogy of philosophy', *Radical Philosophy*, 75 (1996), 44.
[22] Slavoj Žižek, *Organs Without Bodies: Deleuze and Consequences* (London, 2004), pp. 183–4.
[23] Gilles Deleuze, *Essays Critical and Clinical* (London, 1998), p. 135.
[24] See Gilles Deleuze, *Spinoza: Practical Philosophy* (San Francisco, 1988), pp. 20–1.
[25] On Deleuze's critique of Kantian ethics, see most particularly Gilles Deleuze, *Nietzsche and Philosophy* (London, 1986), p. 94. For a good discussion of Deleuze's critical relation to Kant, see Iain Mackenzie, *The Idea of Pure Critique* (London, 2004), pp. 1–14. Also, see the first part of chapter 6.
[26] On the decidedly ideological nature of the 'pre-ideological real', see Paul Ricoeur, *Hermeneutics and the Human Sciences* (Cambridge, 1981), p. 230.
[27] This is a point that I take up in slightly different way in R. Porter, 'A world beyond ideology?: strains in Slavoj Žižek's ideology critique', in Malesevic and Mackenzie (eds), *Ideology After Poststructuralism*, p. 50 and p. 62. Also see R. Porter, 'Ideology', in Mackenzie (ed.), *Political Concepts*, p. 535.
[28] See Michael Freeden, *Ideologies and Political Theory: A Conceptual Approach* (Oxford, 1996), p. 29.
[29] Ibid., pp. 94–5.
[30] I am grateful to Howard Williams for pointing this out to me.
[31] See E. Laclau, 'Deconstruction, pragmatism, hegemony', in C. Mouffe (ed.), *Deconstruction and Pragmatism* (London, 1996), p. 53.
[32] Ernesto Laclau and Chantal Mouffe, *Hegemony and Socialist Strategy: Towards a Radical Democratic Politics* (London, 1985), p. 193.
[33] For an analysis of Laclau and Mouffe that tries to tease out the moral or ethical implications of their 'radical' democratic theory, see Anne Marie Smith, *Laclau and Mouffe: The Radical Democratic Imaginary* (London, 1998), p. 177.
[34] 'The reality of the situation' is a particularly prominent trope in the professional political discourse of Northern Ireland. In using this trope, the Northern Ireland politician will typically run together her or his analysis of political events (whether a Unionist, Nationalist, Republican or Loyalist interpretation) with the posited real or 'reality', the latter being merely reflected in the interpretation itself. For a good appreciation and analysis of how ideology functions in actual, everyday social and political discourse, see, for example, M. Billig, 'Ideology, language and discursive psychology', in Malesevic and Mackenzie (eds), *Ideology After Poststructuralism*, pp. 134–56.

Bibliography

Adam, B., Beck, U. and Van Loon, J. (eds), *The Risk Society and Beyond* (London, 2000).
Althusser, L., 'Ideology and ideological state apparatuses', in S. Žižek (ed.), *Mapping Ideology* (London, 1994), pp. 100–40.
Ansell Pearson, K., *Germinal Life: The Difference and Repetition of Deleuze* (London, 1999).
Apel, K. O., 'Openly strategic uses of language: a transcendental-pragmatic perspective', in P. Dews (ed.), *Habermas: A Critical Reader* (Oxford, 1999), pp. 272–90.
Auster, P., *The New York Trilogy* (London, 1987).
Billig, M., 'Ideology, language and discursive psychology', in S. Malesevic and I. Mackenzie (eds), *Ideology After Poststructuralism* (London, 2002), pp. 134–56.
Bordwell, D. and Thompson, K., *Film Art: An Introduction* (New York, 2004).
Boundas, C. V., 'Serialization and subject-formation', in C. V. Boundas and D. Olkowski (eds), *Gilles Deleuze and the Theater of Philosophy* (New York, 1994), pp. 99–116.
Colebrook, C., *Gilles Deleuze* (London, 2002).
Coole, D., 'The dialectics of the real', in S. Malesevic and I. Mackenzie (eds), *Ideology After Poststructuralism* (London, 2002), pp. 111–33.
Craine, J. and Aitken, S. C., 'Street fighting: placing the crisis of masculinity in David Fincher's *Fight Club*', *GeoJournal*, 59, 4 (2004), 289–96.
Deleuze, G., *Nietzsche and Philosophy* (London, 1986).
Deleuze, G., *Foucault* (Minneapolis, 1988).
Deleuze, G., *Spinoza: Practical Philosophy* (San Francisco, 1988).
Deleuze, G., *Cinema 2: The Time-Image* (London, 1989).
Deleuze, G., *Empiricism and Subjectivity: An Essay on Hume's Theory of Human Nature* (New York, 1991).
Deleuze, G., *Cinema 1: The Movement-Image* (London, 1992).
Deleuze, G., *Expressionism in Philosophy: Spinoza* (New York, 1992).
Deleuze, G., *The Fold: Leibniz and the Baroque* (London, 1993).
Deleuze, G., *Negotiations* (New York, 1995).
Deleuze, G., *Essays Critical and Clinical* (London, 1998).
Deleuze, G., 'Having an idea in cinema', in E. Kaufman and K. J. Heller (eds), *Deleuze and Guattari* (Minneapolis, 1998), pp. 14–19.
Deleuze, G. and Guattari, F., *Anti-Oedipus: Capitalism and Schizophrenia* (London, 1984).

Deleuze, G. and Guattari, F., *A Thousand Plateaus: Capitalism and Schizophrenia* (London, 1988).
Deleuze, G. and Guattari, F., *What is Philosophy?* (London, 1994).
Deleuze, G. and Parnet, C., *Dialogues* (London, 1987).
Dews, P. (ed.), *Habermas: A Critical Reader* (Oxford, 1999).
Freeden, M., *Ideologies and Political Theory: A Conceptual Approach* (Oxford, 1996).
Garnham, N., 'The media and the public sphere', in C. Calhoun (ed.), *Habermas and the Public Sphere* (London, 1992), pp. 359–76.
Goodchild, P., *Deleuze and Guattari: An Introduction to the Politics of Desire* (London, 1996).
Habermas, J., *Communication and the Evolution of Society* (London, 1979).
Habermas, J., *The Theory of Communicative Action Vol. 1: Reason and the Rationalization of Society* (London, 1984).
Habermas, J., *Moral Consciousness and Communicative Action* (Cambridge, 1990).
Habermas, J., *The Philosophical Discourse of Modernity* (Cambridge, 1990).
Habermas, J., *The Structural Transformation of the Public Sphere* (Cambridge, 1992).
Habermas, J., *The Past as Future* (Cambridge, 1994).
Habermas, J., *The Habermas Reader* (Cambridge, 1996).
Habermas, J., *Postmetaphysical Thinking* (Cambridge, 1998).
Habermas, J., 'Richard Rorty's pragmatic turn', in R. Brandom (ed.), *Rorty and his Critics* (Oxford, 2000), pp. 31–55.
Habermas, J., *The Future of Human Nature* (Cambridge, 2003).
Hardt, M., *Gilles Deleuze: An Apprenticeship in Philosophy* (London, 1993).
Hardt, M., 'The withering of civil society', in E. Kaufman and K. J. Heller (eds), *Deleuze and Guattari* (Minneapolis, 1998), pp. 23–39.
Hobbes, T., *Leviathan* (London, 1968).
Hoberman, J., 'Under the rainbow', *Sight and Sound*, 9, 1 (1999), 14–16.
Jameson, F., 'Postmodernism and the market', in Slavoj Žižek (ed.), *Mapping Ideology* (London, 1994), pp. 278–95.
Kant, I., *Groundwork of the Metaphysic of Morals* (New York, 1964).
Kant, I., 'What is enlightenment?', in S. Lotringer and L. Hochroth (eds), *The Politics of Truth: Michel Foucault* (New York, 1995), pp. 7–20.
Kay, S., *Žižek: A Critical Introduction* (Cambridge, 2003).
Laclau, E., 'Deconstruction, pragmatism, hegemony', in C. Mouffe (ed.), *Deconstruction and Pragmatism* (London, 1996), pp. 47–68.
Laclau, E. and Mouffe, C., *Hegemony and Socialist Strategy: Towards a Radical Democratic Politics* (London, 1985).
Lecercle, J. J., 'The pedagogy of philosophy', *Radical Philosophy*, 75 (1996), 43–4.
Lyotard, J. F., *The Postmodern Condition: A Report on Knowledge* (Manchester, 1994).

Mackenzie, I., 'Creativity as criticism: the philosophical constructivism of Deleuze and Guattari', *Radical Philosophy*, 86 (1997), 7–18.
Mackenzie, I., *The Idea of Pure Critique* (London, 2004).
Malesevic, S. and Mackenzie, I. (eds), *Ideology After Poststructuralism* (London, 2002).
Marx, K. and Engels, F., *The German Ideology* (London, 1974).
Massumi, B., *A User's Guide to Capitalism and Schizophrenia: Deviations from Deleuze and Guattari* (London, 1993).
McCarthy, T., *The Critical Theory of Jürgen Habermas* (Cambridge, 1984).
Moriarty, M., 'Žižek, religion and ideology', *Paragraph*, 24 (2001), 125–39.
Olsen, M., 'Singing in the rain', *Sight and Sound*, 10, 3 (2000), 26–8.
O'Neill, S., *Impartiality in Context: Grounding Justice in a Pluralist World* (New York, 1997).
Outhwaite, W., *Habermas: A Critical Introduction* (Cambridge, 1994).
Patton, P., *Deleuze and the Political* (London, 2000).
Plato, *The Republic* (London, 1975).
Porter, R., 'Deleuze, geophilosophy, criticism' (unpublished Ph.D. thesis, Queens University, Belfast, 1999).
Porter, R., 'A world beyond ideology?: strains in Slavoj Žižek's ideology critique', in S. Malesevic and I. Mackenzie (eds), *Ideology After Poststructuralism* (London, 2002), pp. 43–63.
Porter, R., 'The singularity of the political', in A. Finlayson and J. Valentine (eds), *Politics and Post-structuralism* (Edinburgh, 2002), pp. 193–205.
Porter, R., 'Ideology', in I. Mackenzie (ed.), *Political Concepts: A Reader and a Guide* (Edinburgh, 2005), pp. 525–52.
Porter, R. and Porter, K. A., 'Habermas and the pragmatics of communication: a Deleuze-Guattarian critique', *Social Semiotics*, 13, 2 (2003), 129–45.
Ricoeur, P., *Hermeneutics and the Human Sciences* (Cambridge, 1981).
Rorty, R., *Contingency, Irony and Solidarity* (Cambridge, 1989).
Rorty, R., 'Feminism, ideology and deconstruction: a pragmatist view', in Slavoj Žižek (ed.), *Mapping Ideology* (London, 1994), pp. 227–34.
Rorty, R., 'Universality and truth', in R. Brandom (ed.), *Rorty and his Critics* (Oxford, 2000), pp. 1–30.
Smith, A. M., *Laclau and Mouffe: The Radical Democratic Imaginary* (London, 1998).
Smith, D., 'The place of ethics in Deleuze's philosophy', in E. Kaufman and K. J. Heller (eds), *Deleuze and Guattari* (Minneapolis, 1998), pp. 251–69.
Susser, B., 'The domains of ideological discourse', *The Journal of Political Ideologies*, 1, 2 (1996), 165–81.
Taubin, A., 'So good it hurts', *Sight and Sound*, 9, 11 (1999), 16–18.
Taylor, C., *Multiculturalism and the Politics of Recognition* (New Jersey, 1992).
Thompson, J., *Ideology and Modern Culture: Critical Social Theory in the Era of Mass Communication* (Cambridge, 1990).

Williams, C., 'Ideology and imaginary: returning to Althusser', in S. Malesevic and I. Mackenzie (eds), *Ideology After Poststructuralism* (London, 2002), pp. 28–42.
Williams, H., *Kant's Political Philosophy* (Oxford, 1983).
Williams, H., *Concepts of Ideology* (Sussex, 1988).
Žižek, S., *The Sublime Object of Ideology* (London, 1989).
Žižek, S., 'Beyond discourse analysis', in E. Laclau, *New Reflections on the Revolution of Our Time* (London, 1990).
Žižek, S., *For They Know Not What They Do: Enjoyment as a Political Factor* (London, 1991).
Žižek, S., *Tarrying with the Negative: Kant, Hegel and the Critique of Ideology* (Durham, 1993).
Žižek, S. (ed.), *Mapping Ideology* (London, 1994).
Žižek, S., *The Indivisible Remainder: An Essay on Schelling and Related Matters* (London, 1996).
Žižek, S., *The Abyss of Freedom* (Michigan, 1997).
Žižek, S., *The Plague of Fantasies* (London, 1997).
Žižek, S., *The Ticklish Subject* (London, 1999).
Žižek, S., *The Art of the Ridiculous Sublime* (Seattle, 2000).
Žižek, S., *The Fragile Absolute* (London, 2000).
Žižek, S., *Did Some Say Totalitarianism?: Five Interventions in the (Mis)use of a Notion* (London, 2001).
Žižek, S., *On Belief* (London, 2001).
Žižek, S., *Organs Without Bodies: Deleuze and Consequences* (London, 2004).

Index

Althusser, Louis 58, 59–60, 62, 63, 68, 69, 72
American Declaration of Independence 6
antagonism 11, 12, 53, 55–6, 57, 66–7, 70, 72, 73, 87, 133
anti-abortionism 56, 57, 67
Anti-Oedipus 11, 86, 89–91, 98–100
anti-Semitic paranoia 54–6, 57, 58, 66–7, 69, 70, 77, 87, 133
Austin, John 37
autonomy, individual 13, 15, 25–6, 44, 51, 84, 88, 92, 119, 120, 121, 123, 135, 137
autonomy, moral 15, 17, 44–50, 135

Badiou, Alain 58, 60–1, 63, 68, 69, 83
Beck, Ulrich 81
Blair, Tony 75, 76

Capital 80
capitalism 7–8, 76, 82, 91, 100, 103, 105, 116, 128, 129, 130
cinema 17, 93–7, 105, 106–11; see also film
Cinema 1: The Movement-Image 93
Cinema 2: The Time-Image 105, 106
class relations 4–5, 91
Clinton, Bill 57, 76
communication 10–11, 23–4, 27–8, 42, 44, 45, 49, 51
communicative action 30–1, 36–40, 45–6, 49, 51, 86–7, 92, 120–1, 122–4, 125, 126, 133
consumerism 13, 32–4, 42, 87, 133, 135, 137
contextualism 20, 22–3, 24

continuing education 104–5
control societies 103, 104–5
cynicism, ideology of 73, 74, 80–4

de Tracy, Antoine Destutt 2–3
Deleuze, Gilles 1, 2, 9, 10, 11–12, 13, 15, 16, 17, 24, 31, 34, 85, 86–102, 103–16, 117, 122–8, 128–31, 132, 134, 135, 136, 137
conception of the real 11, 127–8, 129
desire, theory of 11–12, 13, 15, 86–91, 98–102, 103, 105, 106–16, 126–8, 129, 130, 132, 133, 135
ethical theory 103–16, 126, 127, 129–30
reason and rationality 86–91, 125–6
subjectivity, theory of 17, 86, 91–8, 106, 137
democratization 62
desire 11–12, 13, 15, 54–5, 67–8, 86, 90–1, 98–102, 103, 105, 106–16, 114–16, 126–8, 129, 130, 132, 133, 135
machinic operation of 89–91, 100–101
Did Somebody Say Totalitarianism? 75
difference 14, 92–8

Either/Or 45
Empiricism and Subjectivity: An Essay on Hume's Theory of Human Nature 92, 93
Engels, Friedrich 2, 3–5, 9
ethical, the, *see* ideology
ethical belief 73, 74, 80–4, 118
ethical responsibility 73, 74

ethics of joy 112–16, 127
Expressions in Philosophy: Spinoza 112

fantasy 52, 53–8, 59, 65–6, 67–8, 69, 70, 72, 81, 82, 84, 87, 118
fascism 13, 55
feminism 14–15, 50
Fight Club 7–8
film 7–8, 17, 106–16; *see also* cinema
Fincher, David 7
Foucault, Michel 98
Freeden, Michael 2, 5, 7–8, 9–10, 12, 13, 14, 15, 132, 133, 134
freedom 72, 74, 80, 81–2, 88, 119, 137
French Revolution, the 61
Freud, Sigmund 54, 99
Freudian theory of desire 11, 54, 86, 98, 99–100
Future of Human Nature, The 41, 43–4

Gallie, W. B. 8
'Genesis of the Self and Social Control, The' 27
German Ideology, The 4–5
Guattari, Félix 11, 86, 89–91, 92, 98–100, 112, 123, 128

Habermas, Jürgen 1, 2, 9, 12–13, 16, 18–35, 36–51, 52, 57, 85, 116, 117, 118–22, 122–8, 130, 131, 132, 134–5, 136
  communication theory 10–11, 23–4, 27, 28, 42, 44, 45, 49, 51, 30–1, 36, 37–40, 45–6, 49, 86–7, 92, 120–1, 122–4, 125, 126, 133
  conception of reason and rationality 19–24, 28, 86–7, 88, 125, 133
  conception of the real 10–11, 12, 18–20, 28–35, 40, 52, 120
  moral and ethical theory 13, 15, 17, 25–6, 27, 28, 32–4, 36, 39, 41–3, 44, 46–51, 87, 119, 120, 121, 122–5, 126, 133, 135, 137
  subjectivity, theory of 19, 24, 25–8, 92, 124

Haider, Jorg 75
'Having an idea in cinema' 105, 106
Hegel, G. W. F. 21–2
Hegemony and Socialist Strategy 136
history 21–2
Hitchcock, Alfred 17, 93, 96, 127
Hobbes, Thomas 41
Hume, David 92–3, 94

Ideologies and Political Theory 7
ideology
  and class relations 4–5
  as 'decontested ordering of the political' 7, 8, 9
  as 'interpretative code' 5–7, 9
  and the moral or ethical 1, 2, 12–15, 16, 36–51, 72–85, 103–16, 117, 118, 126, 128–31, 133–6, 137
  and the real 1, 2–12, 16, 18–35, 52, 65–71, 86, 98–102, 117, 119–20, 121–2, 125, 127, 129, 131–3, 135, 136, 137
'impossible gaze' 56
interpellation 59–60, 68, 69, 72, 78

Kant, Immanuel 21, 45, 76–8, 88–9
Kantianism 22, 31, 45, 77–8, 79, 80, 118, 129, 130–1, 134, 135
Kierkegaard, Søren 44–5, 83, 84
Klee, Paul 106

Lacan, Jacques 11, 52, 58–9, 63, 64, 65, 72, 74, 118
Laclau, Ernesto 15, 135–6
language 11, 23, 25, 27, 28, 36, 37–8, 39, 40, 41–2, 51, 52, 121, 122, 123, 125
Lecercle, Jean-Jacques 128

Magnolia 17, 106–116, 126, 130, 137
Mann, Amiee 109, 113
Marx, Karl 2, 3–5, 9, 80
Marxism 9–10
Mead, George Herbert 25, 27
metaphysical rationalism 23, 24

INDEX

metaphysical thinking 20–4, 25–6; *see also* postmetaphysical thinking
moral, the, *see* ideology
Moral Consciousness and Communicative Action 124
Mouffe, Chantal 135–6
multiculturalism 14

Napoleon I 3
Nazism 13, 77
New Labour 75
New Right populism 75–6
Nietzsche, Friedrich 88, 89
Nietzsche and Philosophy 88
Nietzscheanism 96, 126, 127, 128, 97; *see also* pseudo-Nietzscheanism

objectivism 20
Oedipus complex 98–100, 101
On Belief 81

'Pedagogy of philosophy, The' 128
philosophy of consciousness 26
Plague of Fantasies, The 53
Plato 20–1
Platonism 21, 22
Pleasantville 17, 47–50
'police' logic 62
political concepts 7, 8, 9, 17, 83, 106, 136
political discourse 55, 66–7, 70, 136–7
political life 8, 41, 68, 91
positivism 41
postmetaphysical ethics 44–5
postmetaphysical thinking 23, 24, 25, 27; *see also* metaphysical thinking
'Postscript on control societies' 104
pseudo-Nietzscheanism 94, 95, 96, 101, 103, 116
psychoanalysis 11, 52, 54, 58–9, 63, 64, 72, 89–90, 91, 99, 108, 118

Radical Philosophy 128
Rancière, Jacques 58, 60–3, 68, 69

real, the
 communicative or post-metaphysical conception of 10–11, 12, 18–20, 28–35, 40, 52
 pre-ideological or non-ideological 1, 19, 101, 131, 132–3, 136, 137
 psychoanalytically inflected conception of 11, 12, 52, 53, 58–9, 63, 64, 65–71, 72, 118
 and ideology, *see* ideology
 'desire' and the 'social field' 11, 98–102, 127–8, 129
Real, the 11, 12, 16, 52–3, 64–71, 72–4, 80, 84, 85, 118, 119–20
reason, rationality 19–24, 29, 49–50, 53, 56–8, 67, 68–9, 70, 86–91, 125–6, 133
 cynical reason 80, 81, 84; *see also* cynicism, ideology of
 psychoanalytical reason 91, 100; *see also* psychoanalysis
repression 11–12, 13, 17, 100, 103, 105, 108, 109, 111, 116, 126, 130, 135
Ricoeur, Paul 2, 5–7, 9, 10, 12, 132, 133
risk society 82
Rope 17, 93–7, 101, 102, 103, 127
Ross, Gary 17, 47

'Science and Ideology' 5
scientism 36, 40–6, 87
self, the
 autonomy of 13, 15, 17, 25–6, 27, 28, 39, 40, 44, 45, 47, 51, 119, 124
 intersubjectivistic conception of 25, 26–7, 28–9, 45–6, 54
 relation to 'the other' 14, 25, 26, 27, 54–5, 64, 107, 119
Singer, Bryan 17, 63, 83, 137
social field 11, 55, 100, 101, 102, 103, 114, 127
social life 8, 41, 54, 66, 89, 90, 91, 100, 122, 133
social meaning 65, 66

social order 61, 62, 66
social reality 4, 10, 11, 18, 28–2, 34, 52, 67, 69–70, 71, 81, 87, 91, 100, 101, 122, 132, 133
social reciprocity 13, 15, 39, 40, 51, 120, 121, 123
social relations 32, 34, 42, 51, 57, 114, 120–1, 122, 128
social world 6–7, 11, 27, 51, 53, 57, 64, 66, 70, 73, 87, 101, 103, 127, 131–2, 133
speech acts 37–9, 40, 51, 120, 123, 124, 125
Spinoza, Baruch 111–12, 128
Spinoza: Practical Philosophy 111
Spinozism 116, 126, 127, 128, 130, 133, 134, 137
state, the 60–3, 68, 83
Structural Transformation of the Public Sphere, The 32, 34
subjective destitution 53, 59, 63–4, 68, 69, 83, 84, 119
subjectivity 17, 48, 49, 53, 58–65, 67, 68, 69, 72, 83, 86, 91–8, 106, 124, 137
subjectivization 53, 58, 59–63, 68, 69
Sublime Object of Ideology, The 69
Susser, Bernard 13
symbolic, the 52–3, 63, 64, 65–7, 68–70, 72, 73–4, 78, 83, 119

Tarrying with the Negative 128
Taylor, Charles 14
technocratic consciousness 13, 41–3, 51, 135
technology 13, 36, 40–6, 87
Theory and Practice 41
Theory of Communicative Action, The 37

Thomas Anderson, Paul 17, 106–111, 114–15, 126, 137
Thousand Plateaus, A 98, 123
Ticklish Subject, The 59
Toward a Rational Society 41
totalitarianism, ideology of 13, 73, 74, 75–80, 118, 135
tradition, prejudices of 13, 51, 87, 135

United States of America (USA) 6
'Unity of reason in the diversity of its voices, The' 19
Usual Suspects, The 17, 63–4, 68–9, 83, 119, 137

values, critical evaluation of 12, 15, 134–7
vitalism 92, 93, 97, 100–1, 106

What is Philosophy? 128

Žižek, Slavoj 1, 2, 9, 10, 11, 17, 24, 31, 34, 52–71, 72–85, 88, 105, 116, 117, 118–22, 125, 128–32, 133, 134, 135, 136, 137
  concept of reason and rationality 53–8, 67–8, 86, 87
  ethical theory 13, 15, 72–85, 118, 135
  psychoanalytically inflected concepts 11, 12, 53, 54, 65–71, 72, 108
  Real, the 11, 12, 16, 52–3, 64–71, 72–4, 80, 84, 85, 118, 119–20, 133
  subjectivity, theory of 53, 58–65, 67, 68, 69, 72, 83, 84, 119